CHRIST EVANGELICAL BIBLE INSTITUTE

God, Our Universal Self

A Primer for Future Christian Metaphysics

Millennial Edition

Rev. Joseph Adam Pearson, Ph.D.

COPYRIGHT

DEDICATION

This work is dedicated to the human beings who will be alive when the *only-begotten* Son of God, Christ Jesus, returns to Earth for his Millennial reign of peace. By then, this world will have lost at least one-half of its population from warfare, lawlessness, anarchy, global warming, famine, drought, pestilence, plague, and cataclysmic disaster.

FOREWORD

Dear Readers,

With the publication of this book, I have completed my trilogy on fundamental Christian metaphysics.

My first book, entitled *Classroom Version of As I See It: The Nature of Reality by God,* is intended to be read first in the series. It is written as a narrative in the first person singular as if God were writing in order to more fully engage readers in their introduction to Christian metaphysics.

My second book, entitled *Divine Metaphysics of Human Anatomy,* is intended to be read last in the trilogy series. After I finished writing it, I realized that there was a need for a more basic book on Christian metaphysics — a primer of sorts — not for understanding past works on Christian metaphysics by other authors but for future studies on Christian metaphysics that would make it more relatable to, and practical for, students to use during the third millennium of the Christian era.

This current book, entitled *God, Our Universal Self: A Primer for Future Christian Metaphysics,* is meant to be read second in the series — after *Classroom Version of As I See It: The Nature of Reality by God* but before *Divine Metaphysics of Human Anatomy.* Whereas the first book in the trilogy series is meant to help beginning students understand how to look at life from the standpoint of Christian metaphysics, this current book (i.e., the second in the trilogy series) is meant to help the reader think and solve problems daily using Christian metaphysics.

The book *Divine Metaphysics of Human Anatomy* completes the trilogy by presenting a detailed view of human structure and function from the standpoint of contemporary Christian metaphysics; it is intended for advanced students of Christian metaphysics.

All three books in the trilogy will help readers to understand how spiritual reality and physical reality are interwoven. They will also help readers to harmonize contemporary mainstream Christianity with Christian metaphysics by helping them to see that the two perspectives are complementary and not contradictory. Finally, the trilogy will help readers to harmonize Biblical truth with facts and well-grounded theories from the natural sciences. (The only way to harmonize some aspects of the two is through Christian metaphysics.)

I believe that all of my books on Christian metaphysics, including others not in this trilogy series, will be useful not only to Christians before the return of Christ Jesus but also to those living during his Millennial reign on Earth. To my knowledge, my books on Christian metaphysics are the only books that have been written primarily for a readership living during the 1,000 years that Christ Jesus rules on Earth. Any adjustments that need to be made in the presentation of the concepts contained within any of my books will be made under the direction of Christ Jesus himself during his Millennial rule. All authentic practitioners of Christian metaphysics must always defer to the sovereignty of Christ Jesus and the supremacy of God's absolute truth.

I pray that readers take the truths contained within my books to heart, that the truths help them to grow spiritually, and that they are inspired to impartially discuss, respectfully debate, and courteously share these truths with others.

Much love in Jesus Christ,

Joseph Adam Pearson

Rev. Joseph Adam Pearson, Ph.D.

NOTES

As used in this book, *KJV* is an abbreviation for the public domain *King James Version* of the Holy Bible. To ensure their accuracy throughout this book, all paraphrases of the public domain *King James Version* of the Holy Bible were finalized only after first checking: (1) the Masoretic Hebrew text of the Tanakh (the Jewish Bible) for accuracy of passages from the *KJV Old Testament* and (2) the earliest Greek text extant for accuracy of passages from the *KJV New Testament.* Additionally, to enhance readability of the public domain *KJV* text, archaic English words like *hath, thou,* and *ye* have been changed to their modern equivalents.

Most transliterated Hebrew and Greek words referenced within the text of this book are noted by their respective numbers [in brackets with a preceding "H" for Hebrew or "G" for Greek] from the *Dictionary of the Hebrew Bible* and the *Dictionary of the Greek Bible* found in *Strong's Exhaustive Concordance of the Bible* by James Strong (Copyright 1890), Crusade Bible Publishers, Inc., Nashville.

Although God the Father (i.e., the *Lord God Almighty)* and God the Son (i.e., the *Lord Jesus Christ)* are consubstantially united in the Godhead along with God the Holy Spirit, in order to distinguish *God the Father* from *God the Son* in this book, an upper case "H" is used for personal pronouns specifically referring to *God the Father (He, His,* and *Him)* and a lower case "h" is used for personal pronouns specifically referring to *God the Son (he, his,* and *him).*

Clarification: The word *consubstantial* — meaning "having the same nature and essence and, therefore, made of the same substance" — has been translated from ὁμοούσιον *(homoousion),* the accusative case form of the Greek word ὁμοούσιος *(homoousios).* The word *co-essential* is also translated from the Greek word ὁμοούσιος *(homoousios)* and has two different senses, imports, or significations: (1) "of equal importance" *(meaning a)* as well as (2) "having the same nature and essence and, therefore, made of the same substance" *(meaning b).* In relation to the Godhead, *nature, substance,* and *essence* denote Spirit (i.e., the nature, substance, or essence of the Supreme Being) and are used synonymously in this book; they describe *spiritual/invisible nature, spiritual/invisible substance,* and *spiritual/invisible essence* — in contrast to words that describe *physicality, materiality, corporeality, matter,* and *physical energy.*

Whenever the word *God* is used in this book (i.e., with an upper case "G"), the reader should assume that the word is referring to the God of the Holy Bible — who is the *Lord God Almighty* or *Yahweh* (YHWH), the one true and only real Creator-God.

Although the Creator-God does not possess a human gender, there are no apologies for the use of the male pronouns *He, His, and Him* in this book when referring to the Lord God Almighty *(God the Father)* for the following reasons: In general, certain words in theology and philosophy are capitalized to show that they represent qualities and characteristics that transcend human understanding and experience. This includes the pronouns *He, His,* and *Him* and even the word *God* itself. *She* and *Her* are not used in this book when referring to the Creator-God because many people in the early 21st century, if not most people, have a tendency to confuse the use of female pronouns with advocating Wicca and other ancient and modern pagan cults that worship the Mother-Goddess — such as those devoted to Cybele, Aphrodite (Venus), Hecate, Artemis (Diana), Magna Mater, Ma, Anaitis, Ashtoreth (Astarte), Ma'at, Morrigan, etc.

For the sake of clarity, when the author of *God, Our Universal Self* uses the phrase *the present author,* he is referring to himself.

TABLE OF CONTENTS

Copyright ii

Dedication iii

Foreword v

Notes..vii

Table of contents...ix

Introduction..xiii

    Exercises and Activities......................................xviii

Chapter One: On Being Our *Self*...................................1

  Jesus Christ, the Great I AM 1

  The Role of Powerful Emotions 11

  Discovery, Control, and Discipline in
      Relationship to *Self*...12

  ego-centrism versus *Ego-centrism* 19

  Losing Ourselves to Find Our *Self*.........................23

  Our God, Our *Self*...25

  Healing Metaphysically...26

  Exercises and Activities 28

Chapter Two: Preparing to Meet Our *Self* 31

Being Who We Really Are 31

The Holy and the Vulgar 33

Entering into Temptation 35

Beside Our *Self* 38

When Satan becomes our *self* 39

Our One True and Only Real Enemy 40

The Portal to a Hellish State of Existence 46

"Who Am I?" 50

Forgiving Ourselves 52

Spiritual Provisions during Faith Development 53

Exercises and Activities 56

Chapter Three: States of Mind 61

Definitions 61

Satan's Mortal Mind 69

God's Divine Mind 70

The Power of Chronic Physical Pain 73

Exercises and Activities 76

Chapter Four: Whom Shall We Seek to Please? 79

Control and Possession 79

Exercises and Activities 84

Chapter Five: The Quest for Harmony 87

    Genesis and the Natural Sciences 87

    Thinking Metaphysically 94

    Resolving Problems Metaphysically 99

    Exercises and Activities 109

Chapter Six: The Will of Our Universal Self 111

    The Supremacy and Sovereignty of God's Will ... 111

    How to Combat Satan's Mortal Mind 119

    Pondering Victory 122

    Exercises and Activities 126

Chapter Seven: Every Thing is a Function of Consciousness 129

    Exercises and Activities 138

Afterword 141

Appendix 143

Books by the Author 145

About the Author 147

Introduction

Metaphysics describes the nature of reality. *Christian metaphysics* describes the nature of spiritual reality from the standpoint of salvation through Jesus Christ. *Metaphysics* resolves things into thoughts and thoughts into things. *Christian metaphysics* accomplishes the same thing except that every view is filtered through the spiritual lens of the Holy Bible with all hindsight, insight, and foresight provided by the only teacher of all truth, the Creator-God's Holy Spirit. Thinking metaphysically for Christians requires holding the whole spiritual truth while simultaneously attending to its various parts. Thinking metaphysically for Christians also requires looking beyond corporeality and physical explanations to spirituality and supernatural explanations for understanding how to resolve life's challenges. Like two of my previous books,[1] *God, Our Universal Self* is a book on Christian metaphysics; it is intended to be used as a primer for future studies on — as well as practical applications of — Christian metaphysics. This book is written especially for people living during the Millennial Rule of Christ Jesus on Earth.

How can you, the reader or listener, fully learn how to think, speak, and write in the style of Christian metaphysics? You must first learn the Holy Bible backwards and forwards over many years if not over many decades. At the same time, you need to allow spiritual ideas, images, concepts, and conclusions to take shape within your consciousness and seek to articulate them clearly in spoken and written forms. As you deliver and refine your spoken words — and as you write, rewrite, and edit your ideas, images, concepts, and conclusions — you must always compare and contrast what you think, say, and write to the spiritual truths and principles you have learned

---

[1] *Classroom Version of As I See It: The Nature of Reality by God* by Rev. Joseph Adam Pearson, Ph.D., Christ Evangelical Bible Institute, Copyright 2019. ISBN 978-1734294705; and *Divine Metaphysics of Human Anatomy* by Rev. Joseph Adam Pearson, Ph.D., Christ Evangelical Bible Institute, Copyright 2018. ISBN 978-0985772819.

from (and continue to learn from) the Holy Bible. If your spiritual ideas, images, concepts, and conclusions are not complementary to the contextualized truths and principles in the Holy Bible, then you must discard them.

Conscientious students of Christian metaphysics should not only look to harmonize their spiritual ideas, images, concepts, and conclusions with the spiritual truths and principles in the Holy Bible, they should also seek to harmonize anthropology, archeology, astronomy, biology, chemistry, geology, and physics with the Genesis account of creation without worrying that their faith will be found wanting or that they are being disrespectful to Scripture. (For the sake of clarity, the Creator-God's Holy Bible is the only real Scripture.) As a cautionary note here, finding such harmonization does not require that students try to find natural causes for the supernatural and miraculous events recorded in the Holy Bible.

God gave you a superior intellect. Don't be afraid to use it. But never think yourself to be something when you are not — which is to say, dare only to approach the mind of the Creator-God and His Supraconsciousness in humility and gratitude without an iota of arrogance. It is through such an approach that you will experience and know absolute truth for yourself. Don't delay. Answers to questions that you have are waiting to be unlocked from within.

Once you know something by experiencing it, you can never *unknow* it. Although you might try to *not* know it, you will always know it. This is true for everything, including one's personal knowledge of evil from disobeying God. Although Adam and Eve, and their progeny through them, came to know evil experientially from their disobedience to God, through the shed blood of Jesus Christ — God's only-begotten Son — human beings can become holy and pure again; thereafter, they will no longer require being evil by disobeying God in order to recognize that evil can exist or to discern where and when it exists.

The opportunity to have learned what evil is by experiencing it firsthand has proven invaluable to fallen created beings who have since received salvation by accepting the Lord Jesus Christ as their personal Savior. In a way, saved created beings are now more like their Creator than ever because they know the difference between good and evil. At one time, only the Creator could know what evil is. Because the Creator is omniscient, He did not need to become evil in order for Him to recognize evil or know where and when it exists. Created beings, however, could only learn what evil is by disobeying God and, thereby, experiencing evil firsthand. If now saved, such created beings will always remember what evil felt like because they have experienced it for themselves. Consequently, they will never again fall to evil because, sooner or later, saved people make a conscious decision to never again disobey the Will of God. Saved people choose to no longer entertain and indulge unclean desires because they have decided to follow Jesus Christ not only throughout the rest of their earthly lives but also throughout all eternity as well. Although it may take a long time to finally make the commitment to live the rest of your life in honor of Jesus Christ, all people who belong to the Creator-God eventually make that decision as they mature spiritually.

Like His creation, the Creator-God evolves and will continue to evolve, and we will continue to evolve with Him. Before the Logos came to Earth as God the Son, the Godhead had never experienced temptation before. Because the Creator-God is omniscient, He knew what temptation was, and is, and could have dictated a perfectly accurate 100,000 volume encyclopedia about it. But the Creator-God's knowledge of temptation was only academic — which is to say, it was not experiential (i.e., personal and intimate by having been tempted Himself). However, through the experiences of Christ Jesus, the Creator-God's knowledge of temptation is now not only academic but also experiential as well: What God the Son learned about temptation while he was in corporeality was shared synchronously and simultaneously throughout the Godhead. (For the sake of clarity, the tripartite, unified Godhead includes God the Father, God the Son, and God the Holy Spirit.)

The Creator-God evolves Himself. He evolves His creation. He evolves His created beings. He even evolves our human understanding of Him. The Creator-God is neither too big for human beings to understand nor too small for them to overlook. He is just the right size. By permitting us to experience and overcome evil for ourselves, He brought us closer to His divine level of knowledge and understanding. Although we can never become the Creator-God, we can become more like Him and, thereby, make a more suitable eternal companion for Him — individually, collectively, and corporately.

By permitting Himself to experience temptation through the human experiences of God the Son, God the Father also brought Himself closer to us in His empathy for us. Through the life experiences of Jesus Christ, the entire Godhead now knows experientially what it means to be vulnerable to temptation while in flesh. As God-in-flesh, Christ Jesus himself was touched with and by our infirmities (Matthew 8:17; Hebrews 4:15). To be sure, the Creator-God's eternal mercy flows to us first and foremost through the shed blood of His only-begotten Son, but it is also effluent because of His firsthand understanding of our condition in corporeality — learned through the earthly experiences of His only-begotten Son. The entire Godhead experienced temptation, victimization, and the shedding of innocent blood personally through God the Son.

That the Creator-God evolves and will continue to evolve is not in conflict with the truth that God never changes. To be sure, the Creator-God's substance, nature, and essence never change, but He continues to consciously expand and evolve the substance, nature, and essence of His Being. The Creator-God is ever-expansive experientially. If you think about it, this is what we should expect from a Godhead that is dynamic and not static. His divine Mind remains insatiably inquisitive and curious at the same time that it is creative. The Creator-God continues to create and expand Himself into His ever-expanding spiritual universe. The totality of an ever-evolving and ever-expanding Creator-God can only fit into the totality of an ever-evolving and ever-expanding Creation.

For readers or listeners who may feel offended on behalf of the Creator-God because the present author has stated that His divine

Mind is "insatiably inquisitive and curious," and who feel that this statement is inconsistent with His omniscience, please know that the Creator-God endowed created beings with free will so that He might interact *with* them as well as be challenged *by* them. The Creator-God was not going to be content with just observing His created beings; He wanted, and continues to want, to interact with them. To be sure, the Creator-God wants an eternal companion in us all individually, collectively, and corporately, but He does not want His eternal companion to be predictable, mechanical, and robotic. It pleases the Creator-God to interact with the creativity with which He has endowed us, especially when that creativity is used to honor Him by reflecting and magnifying Him. Indeed, the Creator-God is the original and ongoing source of all of our individual, collective, and corporate creativity.

The Creator-God evolves but does not devolve. Unlike the fallen members of His original creation, the Creator-God cannot devolve. Devolution can only occur in segments, aspects, and parts of His creation when created beings consciously choose to depart from the Creator-God by stepping outside of His Will through disobedience. Of course, devolution happened to Lucifer and the angels who fell with him as well as to the fallen Adamic race; and devolution continues to happen to the spirits of human beings who consciously (i.e., willfully) reject the Creator-God by rejecting His Plan of Salvation and, thereby, continue to disobey His Supreme and Sovereign Will. As a result of their irrevocable rejection of God the Son, the souls of all eternally-reprobate human beings become the *demons, devils,* and *unclean spirits* described in the Holy Bible (all three terms are used synonymously within this book as well as throughout the various translations of the Holy Bible).

Once we know the Creator-God through the shed blood of Christ Jesus, we can never *unknow* Him although we can stop experiencing His goodness and mercy. Through the shed blood of Christ Jesus, the Creator-God becomes and remains our universal Self, Selfhood, Essence, and Being. As free-will beings created by the Creator-God, we can choose to evolve and expand along with Him and become what He would have us become, or we can resolutely choose to disobey Him — in which case, we still know who the Creator-God is but not by being part of Him. Then, the Creator-God's Glory, or Fiery Presence, becomes a terror to us and our separation from Him becomes an eternal nightmare filled only with the spiritual horror that permanently eludes light, forgiveness, hope, joy, and love.

Without God, there is nothing. Outside of God, there can be nothing. To be sure, the nothingness outside of God is something that those committed to Jesus Christ will never need or want to experience again after their full restoration to the Kingdom of God, a heavenly state of *being*.

Exercises and Activities in Christian Metaphysics

1. Name at least one non-Christian philosopher whose expertise was in the field of metaphysics. Briefly describe his or her contributions to the field of metaphysics.

2. Name at least one Christian theologian whose expertise was in the area of Christian metaphysics. Briefly describe his or her contributions to the area of Christian metaphysics.

3. Compare and contrast non-Christian metaphysics with Christian metaphysics by listing three similarities and three differences.

4. Most Christian theologians understand what it means to harmonize the four gospels as well as harmonize the journeys and epistles of the Apostle Paul, but relatively few understand the possibility of harmonizing well-grounded scientific theories and established facts in anthropology, archeology, astronomy, biology, chemistry,

geology, and physics with the Genesis account of creation. Speculate as to how at least one seemingly-contradictory scientific theory or fact can be harmonized with the Genesis account of creation.

5. What are the spiritual benefits from the Adamic Fall? Please explain.

6. The Holy Bible is clear that God does not change. Is the statement "God evolves" contradictory to the truth that "God does not change"? Why or why not?

7. The Holy Bible is very clear that God cannot be tempted and yet the Holy Bible is also very clear that God the Son was tempted. Are these two Biblical truths contradictory? Why or why not? Please explain.

8. Can the Creator-God ever devolve? Why or why not?

9. In Christian metaphysics, the words "nothing" and "nothingness" are meant to convey something different than when they are used in standard speech, colloquial speech, or traditional writing. What do you think "nothing" and "nothingness" mean in Christian metaphysics?

10. Complete the following sentence:
    Something is nothing when _____.

Chapter One

On Being Our *Self*

Jesus Christ, the Great I AM

Jesus Christ, *Christ Jesus*, *Jesus the Christ*, and *Y'shua H'Moshiach* are all synonymous names for the only Messiah of Israel and one true Savior of the world.

Jesus

To use the word *Jesus* alone when referring to the Messiah and Savior is insufficient because there are ordinary mortals who possess the same name.

Y'shua (Yeshua or Jeshua) [H3442] is a contracted form of Yehoshuah (Jehoshua) [H3091] — of which: (1) "Iesous" Ἰησοῦς is the Ionic Greek form; (2) "Iesus" IESVS is the Classical Latin form; and (3) "Jesus" is the Early Modern English form. (See Table One in the Appendix for all Hebrew words referred to by numbers in brackets in this chapter.)

The Hebrew name Yehoshuah (Jehoshua) [H3091] means "YAH [H3050], or YAHWEH [H3068], is salvation" — which is to say, *"the Self-Existent One, or the Great I AM, is* salvation." YAH is the shortened form of YAHWEH, the Name of God often translated into English as *the LORD* and *Jehovah* (with variations in English that include *Yehowah, Yehoweh, Yehovah,* and *Yehoveh*). The LORD God Almighty clarified to Moses (Moshe) what His primary Name is:

{2} And God spoke to Moses, and said to him, "I am *the LORD* [Yahweh]: {3} And I appeared to Abraham, to Isaac, and to Jacob, by the name of God Almighty [El-Shaddai], but by my name Jehovah [Yahweh] was I not known to them."

Exodus 6:2-3 KJV Paraphrase [Author's Brackets]

In an earlier communication from God to Moses, when asked for His Name, God replied: "I AM THAT I AM," or EYEH ASHER EYEH [H1961] [H834] [H1961], and "Tell the children of Israel that "I AM," or EYEH [H1961], has sent you" (Exodus 3:14). This declaration is echoed by Christ Jesus in his response to the Jews who questioned his authority: "Before Abraham was, I AM" (John 8:58). Through his response, Christ Jesus clearly identified himself as one with God. Christ Jesus did not say: "Before Abraham, I was" — which is to say, "I existed before Abraham" (although he surely did). In using "I AM," Christ Jesus was conveying: (1) that he exists in a state of *being* where every moment is part of *an eternal now;* and (2) that "God the Son" is fully, completely, and perfectly one with "God the Father" — the Author, or Creator, of all *being* and, therefore, the *Supreme* Being.

The most important Hebrew word particle, base, or stem found in all of the highly personal names for God in the Holy Bible is YAH [H3050] (often germanized or anglicized as JAH). YAH [H3050] and YAHWEH [H3068] are derived from EYEH [H1961], which is sometimes thought of as a tenseless form of the verb "to be" but is, more importantly, its future tense: *I WILL BE.* Thus, God's answer to Moses includes the meaning: "I WILL BE WHAT I WILL BE." In effect, God was saying to us all: "I WILL BECOME WHAT I WILL BECOME" and "I WILL EVOLVE INTO WHAT I CHOOSE TO EVOLVE." The Creator-God does not change His character, nature, personality, substance, or essence; rather, He evolves by expanding Himself into His ever-evolving and ever-expanding creation (metaphysically parabolized by the physically-observable universe). God continues to elaborate on what He created originally. God continues to create. As stated previously in the *Introduction to* this book, God is not static but dynamic. To be sure, God is our Creator, but His creating did not stop with us. God, our universal Self, continues to evolve.

The word *YAH* really means *Be* or *Being* — or, in this case, "the Great I AM" or *Supreme Being.* Because God is God, He will become exactly what He wants to become. God defines Himself. No one else does. And God continues to define Himself. He will become exactly who He will become without direction from anyone or anything else. God evolves, and God continues to evolve His creation as well as Himself. God even evolves us all in our understanding of Him.

God's created beings can choose either (1) to devolve to a lower state by departing from God through disobedience to His Will or (2) to evolve to a higher state by remaining in (or returning to) Him through sustained obedience to His Will.

> Sing unto God, sing praises to His Name: extol Him that rides upon the heavens by His Name JAH [YAH], and rejoice before Him.
>
> *Psalm 68:4 KJV Paraphrase*

Only people who know the God of the Holy Bible personally through the shed blood of Jesus Christ can use the words YAH or YAHWEH without blaspheming, ridiculing, or insulting the Name of God — of course, only *if* they use it reverently. Albeit the expression *"God* damn it" is vulgar, it is not really cursing, or using the Name of God in vain, because the word *God* is not *the Name of God.* But the expression *"YAH* damn it" would be cursing if it were used as an invective with full knowledge of the origin and meaning of the word *YAH.* Of course, falsely attributing to YAH what He is not, what He did not do, and what He did not say or does not want would be blasphemy. *For example,* to say "JAH wants you to enjoy the ganja (i.e., marijuana or cannabis) that He has made" is blasphemy. Indeed, to speak as if you have God on your side when you do not is a form of blasphemy. (God does not support throwing our lives away in the non-medicinal use, or abuse, of any substance.) To say that you have been healed by the

Lord God Almighty when you have not been healed is also blasphemy. Anytime you use *the Name of God* in vain is blasphemy.

Using the name *Jesus Christ* as an expletive is blasphemy, too. The name *Jesus Christ* should always be honored and revered, never dishonored or disrespected. Using stupid, vulgar, or offensive ideas or pictures and linking them to the Savior is blasphemy against *the Name of God.*

Christ

To use the name *Christ* alone when referring to the Savior is insufficient. When used alone, the word *Christ* can accurately imply a spiritual state of mind and a heightened level of consciousness; however, when used alone, the word *Christ* can also inaccurately imply that the spiritual state of mind and heightened level of consciousness can be achieved without accepting the Biblical Jesus as: (1) the only Messiah of Israel, (2) the only true Savior of the world, and (3) one's only personal Savior. Indeed, one cannot have "the Christ," "the mind of Christ," "divine Mind," or "Christ Consciousness" without accepting the shed blood of the only-begotten Son of God as the only sacrifice acceptable to *God the Father* for the remission of our sins and the cancellation of the debt we owe to God for our sins. To be sure, the purpose for the crucifixion of Christ Jesus is his substitutionary atonement to the Creator-God for our sins.

One cannot have "Jesus" without having "the Christ" and one cannot have "the Christ" without having "Jesus." Christians should always cognitively hold the whole name "Jesus the Christ," or "Jesus Christ," while they simultaneously attend to its two parts, "Jesus" and "(the) Christ." The words *Jesus* and *Christ* are inextricably linked together and should rarely be used separately so as not to confuse the hearer, the reader, or even oneself (yes, we can easily confuse ourselves). The English word *Christ* is a title derived from the Greek word *Christos* Χριστός and its counterpart in Latin, *Christus* CHRISTVS. The Greek word *Christos* Χριστός is one translation of the Hebrew word

4

H'Moshiach [H4899], which means "the Messiah" or "the Anointed One" in English. (The transliterated Greek form of *Moshiach* [H4899] is *Messias* Μεσσίας.)

>>><<<

That both *God the Father* and *God the Son* have the same identity ("I AM") does not mean that they have the same personality or the same function in the universe even though they both have the same purpose and are consubstantial parts of the Godhead along with *God the Holy Spirit.* Jesus the Christ said: "I and my Father are one" (John 10:30 KJV) — which is to say: "My *Self* [or *Egō*] and the Father are one." Jesus Christ also said: "my Father is greater than me [or μου]" (John 14:28 KJV). To be sure, God the Father and God the Son are one, and they have the same identity ("I AM"), but they also have *Self*-assigned functions that are different from each other. In order to understand this more fully, the present author recommends that you read his other two books in this trilogy, entitled *Classroom Version of As I See It: The Nature of Reality by God* [2] and *Divine Metaphysics of Human Anatomy*,[3] both of which detail who God is and why God partitioned Himself into a tri-unity. That "God the Father" and "God the Son" are one does not make them exactly the same nor does it make them sequential manifestations of the Godhead. God the Son did not replace God the Father. And God the Holy Spirit did not replace God the Son. The three are eternally synchronous, simultaneous, and synergistic. Christians thinking of God metaphysically requires that they conceptually hold the whole Godhead at the same time that they attend to the Godhead's triadic parts.

---

[2] *Classroom Version of As I See It: The Nature of Reality by God* by Rev. Joseph Adam Pearson, Ph.D., Christ Evangelical Bible Institute, Copyright 2019. ISBN: 978-1734294705.

[3] *Divine Metaphysics of Human Anatomy* by Rev. Joseph Adam Pearson, Ph.D., Christ Evangelical Bible Institute, Copyright 2018. ISBN 978-0985772819

Some people have a problem with the concurrent preexistence of the triadic parts of the Godhead because of their inability to conceptualize the form of the Godhead before creation. However, if they view that the Creator-God (i.e., the Godhead) consciously partitioned Himself into *God the Father, God the Son,* and *God the Holy Spirit* before He began creating the physically-observable universe, then there should be no problem. The Creator-God partitioned Himself into *God the Father* (Yahweh or "the LORD"), *God the Son* (the Logos or "the spoken Word"), and *God the Holy Spirit* (Ruach HaKo'desh or "the Holy Ghost") in order to provide for the future return of fallen created beings to Him through His Plan of Salvation. (Yes, God created us even though He knew that we would fall.)

Earlier, the present author capitalized *"Self"* to distinguish it as the sole identity of the Godhead, which consists of God the Father, God the Son, and God the Holy Spirit — the equivalent, consubstantial, and coexistent elements of the one true and only real Supreme Being, Creator, and Lord of the Universe. When "self" (lower case *s*) is used in this work, it refers to the identity and being of individual souls, each originally created with free will — or self-volition — in the perfect image and complete likeness of the Creator-God. When "self" is qualified by the prefix *supra* (i.e., *supraself)* or the adjective *higher* (i.e., *higher self),* it refers to the soul indwelt, infused, and comingled by God, our universal Self.

Because our life is in God and God's life is in us (if we accept the crucifixion of Jesus Christ as the only sacrifice acceptable to God the Father for our sins), God is our universal Self. Although God is our universal Self, created beings are not God's *self* — although as created beings our existence affirms God's existence and creative nature. God is the Creator; we are not the Creator nor can we ever be the Creator — even though the Creator works in and through us. The symphony conductor's baton is not the conductor although it is used as an extension of the conductor. That God is our universal Self does not mean that we become God; it means that God infuses us to fully, completely, and perfectly demonstrate our one true and only real identity in Him through Christ Jesus.

6

How we define *self* depends on a number of factors and how we view those factors.

Some theologian-philosophers contrast "being-in-itself" to the "human self" and would define those two phrases differently than the present author will define them in this work.

In this work, *being-in-itself* is the true essence and absolute identity of the individual *self.* For each created being in corporeality, or fallen created being, the *self* includes: (1) the higher *self, supraself,* or absolute identity we have in God (all three of these terms are used synonymously throughout this work); (2) the human *self,* composite *self,* or conscious functioning *self* (all three of these terms are used synonymously throughout this work); and (3) the animal *self,* lower *self,* or abased *self* (all three of these terms are used synonymously throughout this work). The functions of the human mind postulated by Sigmund Freud — *super-ego, ego,* and *id* — loosely correspond to the *self* as it has just been partitioned here into (1), (2), and (3) with the notable exception that Freud did not accede to the existence of God (Freud was an atheist) and, therefore, would never knowingly ascribe divine qualities of the supernatural, spiritual, or metaphysical to any part of the super-ego.

In the reality of God's spiritual universe, the Creator is the true Self of every created being. Here, the present author expands the definition of "being-in-itself" to refer to "the absolute identity of the individual in the *Great I AM of Being,* which identity is obtained by mortals only when they individually surrender themselves to the spiritual efficacy of the shed blood of Jesus Christ as their sole means for personal salvation." Such surrender causes *mortals* to become *immortals.* The word *immortals* is used here in contradistinction to the eternality of souls. As used in this book, a soul is *eternal* regardless of whether it is in Heaven or Hell; a soul is *immortal* only when it is saved and is already in Heaven or unequivocally destined for Heaven.

Some philosophers would say that the *en soi, essence, noumenon,* or *thing-in-itself* (i.e., Immanuel Kant's *das Ding an sich [selbst]*) is unknowable to the human mind because it cannot be apprehended by the physical senses. Their assessment is correct but the assessment does not account for the supernatural, spiritual, or metaphysical reality that can be apprehended, perceived, discerned, and sensed by saved human beings through God's Holy Spirit, which is imparted to them at the precise moment that they believe in, and on, the reality of Jesus Christ and the spiritual significance of his *Self* and *Being* personally, globally, and universally (individually, collectively, and corporately).

Inner conflict still exists for saved souls who remain in a flesh body even though they are already redeemed by the blood of Jesus Christ. Thoughts of — and ideas from — the lower, animal, or abased self regularly try to recapture our attention; and emotions from the conscious functioning self regularly interfere in our making right decisions. In fact, animal passions and human emotions often prevail by preventing the higher self, or *supraself,* from stepping in and taking over for the conscious functioning self.

When thoughts and feelings from our lower, animal, or abased self try to control us, we must not only ignore them but replace them with thoughts of — and feelings from — our higher self, supraself, or absolute identity in God. We are often plundered spiritually by the thoughts of — and feelings from — a mind set apart from God; however, regardless of how mortal and/or carnal that mind may be, we still have access to the mind of Christ Jesus, or God's divine Mind, by way of God's Holy Spirit indwelling us. Through God's Holy Spirit, we can shift our focus away from thoughts and emotions set apart from God to thoughts and emotions that are part of God.

Physical, emotional, mental, and spiritual challenges, including the inner conflict just described, are used by God to spiritually stretch and tighten us as if we were strings in a spiritual orchestra — so that we might live up to our symphonic potential in Him and, thereby, fulfill our purpose and destiny in Him. Thus harmoniously tuned and spiritually attuned, the truths of our universal Self are able to resonate within us, and throughout *us all,* as we are directed by the Great

Conductor and Master Composer of the Universe, the Creator of all who *really* are.

God the Son prayed that we all be one even as he is one with God the Father (John 17:11). And so we are in the process of becoming one with each other as well as one with him so that, one day, the Great I AM will completely, totally, and unreservedly infuse us with the spiritual molecules of His very Being, which spiritual molecules constitute the substance of His Glory.

The impartation of God's Holy Spirit to us at the precise moment of our salvation presages the impartation of God's glory to us when He releases the *totality* of His Fiery Being *into* us all at the very end of what we now know as physical reality and the very beginning of what we will thereafter always know as spiritual reality. This new reality will become known to us at the end of the Millennium of Christ's reign on Earth — after both World War IV (Revelation 20:7-9) and the Great White Throne Judgment (Revelation 20:11) have taken place — at the time when God creates "a new heaven and a new earth" (Revelation 21:1 KJV). *That* is the time when all creation shall be infused with the actual Being and glorified Presence of God the Father. At that time, we all shall be eternally indivisible from one another as well as permanently indivisible from God. In this way, God becomes, and eternally remains, our universal Self. In this way, we will *be* in the Great I AM and the Great I AM will *be* in us. In this way, God will be our universal Self, our absolute identity, and our being-in-itself.

Some religious Christians go to an extreme when they interpret "the Lord God is *one* Lord" (Deuteronomy 6:4) to mean that "God the Father" *is* "God the Son." Although Jesus Christ is the Son of God (Matthew 16:16), God in the flesh (Colossians 2:9; 1 Timothy 3:16), and one with God the Father (John 17:11), Jesus Christ *is not* God the Father. Although the two are one, they are not the same.

The theological position that *God the Son* replaced *God the Father* is untenable because it is unable to offer a plausible explanation concerning: (1) the synchronous, or simultaneous, presence of *God the*

Father and *God the Son* at the times when *God the Father* proclaimed from Heaven: "This is My beloved Son in whom I am well pleased" (Matthew 3:17 and 17:5 KJV); (2) to whom Jesus Christ was speaking from the cross when he said: "Father, forgive them for they do not know what they do" (Luke 23:34 KJV); and (3) to whom Jesus Christ will deliver the Kingdom after *all* enemies of God have finally been conquered:

> And when all things shall be subdued unto him [God the Son], then shall the Son also himself be subject unto Him [God the Father] that put all things under him [under the feet of God the Son], that God may be all in all.
>
> *1 Corinthians 15:28 [4] KJV [Author's Brackets]*

Jesus Christ is "the Word" and "the Word was God" (John 1:1 KJV), but Jesus Christ is *not* God the Father. The roles of God the Father and God the Son are different although Father and Son are one in the Godhead along with God the Holy Spirit — and all three serve the selfsame purpose albeit with different functions.

To be sure, Christ Jesus ("God the Son") already has all authority and all power in Heaven and on Earth (Matthew 28:27 and Ephesians 1:22), but not every enemy has been finally conquered yet, or "subdued unto him" (1 Corinthians 15:28 KJV). For example, at the time of this updated writing (2022), the end-time Antichrist has not yet been overcome. And mortality, or death itself, remains to be conquered. Scripture teaches that the Antichrist will be thrown into the Lake of Fire at the time of Christ Jesus' return to Earth (Revelation 19:20). Scripture also teaches that death, or mortality, is the final enemy that must and will be overcome (1 Corinthians 15:26) when it — along with Hades (the current holding tank for unsaved souls) — will be thrown into the Lake of Fire at the end of the Great White Throne Judgment (Revelation 20:11-14), during which Judgment all remaining souls will

---

[4] See also Ephesians, Chapter One.

either be assigned eternal redemption or eternal damnation. (Read the section entitled *Pondering Victory* in Chapter Six.)

The expression "I AM" not only conveys Self-existence, or the Being and Eternality of God but also Self-awareness, Self-consciousness, and Self-volition — all three of which the Creator possesses. When God releases the totality of His Being into all creation at the time of the end (1 Corinthians 15:28), all saved will then be able to say "We *ARE* that we *ARE*" because they will then have the Great I AM Himself and the fullness of His Being interfacing them. Today, even though we may be saved and have God's Holy Spirit indwelling us, the totality and fullness of God is not yet infused throughout a completely reunited, reunified, renewed, resurrected, revivified, and reclaimed creation. The totality and fullness of God only fits into the totality and fullness of His Creation.

There is *life*. There is *death*. There is *life after death*. But there is also *life after life after death*, at which time the old fallen creation (i.e., corporeality) will pass away and a completely new creation (i.e., a re-creation) will replace it.

The Role of Powerful Emotions

The human self, conscious functioning self, or composite self (all three of these noun phrases are used synonymously throughout this work) is composed of four elements: spirit (personality), biology (corporeality), reason (intellect), and emotion. The human self, or conscious functioning self, is also called a composite self because the four elements just named are inextricably linked to one another to produce a complete human person ("complete" here is not meant to suggest good health or a perfect state of wholeness).

Although some authors may use such expressions as "spiritual self," "physical self," "rational self," and "emotional self" to discuss components of the complete person, these expressions are misleading because they suggest that four separate selves comprise the human person. The present author acknowledges that: (1) these expressions are not necessarily meant to imply that there are four separate selves and (2) the expressions are often used to distinguish component parts for the purpose of general discussion; however, because the expressions may lead people to conceptualize four separate selves, he will not use the expressions in this book except to acknowledge that they exist elsewhere.

When we experience a problem, our problem is generally not the problem; our emotions usually constitute the real problem. How we respond to difficult situations, challenges, facts, and ideas emotionally constitutes the primary problem. Emotions are our primary problem because emotions are capable of controlling the conscious functioning self so that we are: (1) unable to think or reason clearly; (2) unable to restore our physical bodies to homeostasis (i.e., a *steady state* of physiologic equilibrium); and (3) unable to project our best qualities, highest attributes, and most positive attitudes during times of stress.

Emotions are powerful. We have emotions because the Godhead has emotions and because we were originally made in the complete image and perfect likeness of the Godhead. However, when we fell from our original state of being, that fall corrupted our individual personalities, somatic identities, mental abilities, and emotions. This is why all human beings, individually and collectively, have faulty and unstable emotions.

Discovery, Control, and Discipline in Relationship to *Self*

When the present author found God through Jesus Christ, he not only discovered his true self but he also discovered your true self. Indeed, he discovered for himself our one true and only real *Self*. In the final analysis, the reason that we are not really separate from one another is that we have the same Self. How? As saved created beings, our one true and only real identity is now in God through Christ Jesus. God is our universal Self. That is why, in absolute truth, we all live and move and have our *being* in God.[5]

The words "I AM" are signifiers of *Being* and *Being-in-itself.* Because God is the Great "I AM," God is the source of all being and, therefore, the *cause* of all souls — which is to say, the Creator of all *beings.* For those of us who know Christ Jesus, God is not only *the* Creator, God is *our* Creator. That is why He is acknowledged as *Creator-God* in this book. Indeed, God has also become our *Re-Creator*[6] through the shed blood of Jesus Christ. Our souls have been cleansed of all iniquity and our sins have been forgiven. Our souls have been *made anew, remade, born again,* and *spiritually reborn.*

To discover who we are in God through Jesus Christ enables us to gradually gain self-discipline over the areas in our lives that are ungodly and unholy (and, thus, not perfectly reflective of God). Rapid spiritual growth for any individual should be suspect because it takes time for souls in dust (i.e., human beings): (1) to uncover areas within them that represent a lower, animal, and abased self; (2) to take those areas captive in self-discipline through God's indwelling Holy Spirit; and (3) to permanently place those areas under the feet of Jesus Christ — which is to say, under *his* control, power, and authority.

Many people do not recognize that they have a lower, animal, or abased self nipping at their spiritual heels. In fact, because they think that the lower, animal, or abased self is a part of their true identity and real personhood, they misconclude that the pleasure-seeking desires of that self, including its unbridled libido, should be indulged rather than

---

[5] Acts 17:28, King James Version

[6] Here, *Re-Creator* signifies that God transforms fallen souls back to their original, pristine, and glorious state of being at the exact moment that they accept Christ Jesus as their only sacrifice acceptable to God for their trespasses against Him.

resisted, ignored, and replaced with God-given desires to please Him by fulfilling His Will for us individually, collectively, and corporately.

The three main categories of self mentioned previously are characterized by different desires. The lower, animal, or abased self is characterized by its sole desire for self-gratification. The human, conscious functioning, or composite self is characterized by its sole desire for self-survival. In contrast, our higher self, supraself, or absolute identity in God is characterized by its sole desire to do God's Will and, thereby, please Him even at the expense of forfeiting self-gratification and self-survival.

If we do not learn to discipline ourselves spiritually, supernaturally, and metaphysically, our Creator permits the natural sphere to do it for us (that is, to discipline or regulate us). In other words, impure motives, unholy attitudes, and addictive behaviors are permitted to take their toll on us by causing us to lose what we have in order for us to gain a new respect, appreciation, and gratitude for what we had but lost (even if only temporarily). When the resources God has given to us are diminished by indulging impure motives, unholy attitudes, and addictive behaviors, we are then required by God to swim upstream against a worldly current. Sometimes, we lose personal health, resources, and abilities because we have thrown them away. Life becomes even more difficult than it was before until we learn to surrender ourselves to God and lift God up to the place of worship within us that He deserves — which is at the central core of our very being.

In many ways, our human life is a journey to Self-discovery. And, as we find our one true and only real Self, we recognize that there are other parts of our Self that are part of who we really are, too. These other parts are other souls who also belong to God. We are not really separate from others who belong to God. Belonging to God through Jesus Christ is not like belonging to an organization. Belonging to God is belonging to an organism vis-à-vis a corporate spirituality. The saved of God are all joined together by the shed blood of Jesus Christ.

In order to discover our Self, we need to have self-discipline. The reason that we need to have self-discipline and not self-control is that there really is no such thing as self-control. In other words, self-control does not exist. The reason that self-control does not exist is because self-control would require power and power does not belong to any of us because all power has been given to Christ Jesus and those with whom he, and he alone, *shares* power. We do not "grab" power from Christ Jesus and then go off to exist on our own. He bestows his power upon those whom he will and shares his power with those who are called by his Name and are, therefore, joint-heirs with him.

If someone handed us an electric lamp that was turned on and glowing, and we tried to possess the light of the lamp by yanking it toward ourselves, we might unplug the lamp from its source of power and it would no longer provide light. The same is true for the power of God through Christ Jesus. We cannot yank power from God and expect it to sustain us. We must remain connected to the source of all power at all times. We do not possess, or own, power. Christ Jesus alone owns all power. To be sure, when we remain connected to Christ Jesus, we may call upon his Name to release his power in us and through us.

In one way, there is no such thing as self-discovery or Self-discovery because we cannot discover what God has not called us to discover. We discover only what God unveils and reveals to us. To be sure, we can overlook, not recognize, or trivialize what God has called us to understand, but that does not negate that it is God, and God alone, who unveils and reveals absolute truth to us.

God, and God alone, is the Unveiler and Revealer of absolute truth. We do not wrest knowledge from God; God unveils and reveals knowledge to us in accordance with His Will, which is always pure, and in accordance with His timing, which is always perfect.

We do not discover things that are true about ourselves; God unveils and reveals incrementally to us what we need to know and when we need to know it. Sometimes, we become so surprised by what we learn, we misconclude that we are the originators of the truth and that we are its discoverers. Although we can discover things for ourselves, we cannot discover truths for others because they must come to the place where, and time when, they are ready to understand truth for themselves. We might help to provide some tools to others — and, thereby, influence them positively, but they need to do the work for themselves. God's Holy Spirit does not unveil truth to others through us because God's Holy Spirit must be present within them in order for them to understand truth. There is no intercessor except Christ Jesus; there is no intermediary to God's Holy Spirit except him.

In other words, there is no such thing as self-discovery or Self-discovery because there is only revelation to us from Christ Jesus through God's Holy Spirit.

No one forces healing from God; God heals us through His mercy. When you say that you have been healed by God but have not been healed, you bring dishonor to the Name of the Lord God Almighty. It is important for you to remember that you cannot force God to do anything. You must not state that it is God's Will for you to be healed when you really do not know the Will of God nor His timeline for you personally concerning a particular condition. *Ask* God, but do not *tell* God anything. Moreover, it is important for us to remember that healing does not always result in restoration and rejuvenation; sometimes healing results in our ability to look beyond a physical, mental, or emotional challenge that we have. Indeed, God meets every human need, but God does not always do so in ways that we expect or in ways that we think God should — nor in accordance with a timeline that we establish.

There is a difference between proclaiming "I am whole!" and "I have been healed!" Proclaiming "I am whole!" does not mean that you have already been healed; it means that you are claiming wholeness in the Name of your Lord and Savior, Jesus Christ, and that you are choosing to look beyond a challenging condition. (Metaphysical thinking is a means for looking beyond the physical, material, or corporeal world.) In contrast, proclaiming "I have been healed!" means that you have already experienced restoration and rejuvenation and that your challenge is in the past and no longer part of your present earthly experience.

To be sure, self-discipline exists only because we are able to hold onto the reins of the lower self and the human self through God's indwelling Holy Spirit. It is God's Spirit that permits our supraself (the universal *Self* we have in God through Christ Jesus) to discipline us. In reality, self-control does not exist because the Holy Spirit does not hand the reins of control over to us. However, Self-control does exist. The reins remain connected to Christ Jesus through God's Holy Spirit. Christ Jesus disciplines us through God's Holy Spirit. Christ Jesus has all power. Therefore, it is he who truly holds the reins. To be sure, we may grab onto the reins that he controls in order to experience God's Will and God's Power in our lives, but we never take over the reins for God.

There is no such thing as self-control. There is only self-discipline through God, our universal Self.

If you think that you can correct impure motives, unholy attitudes, and addictive behaviors through self-control, then you are sadly mistaken. Laboring with such faulty assumptions, you are destined for failure. Impure motives, unholy attitudes, and addictive behaviors can only be controlled by the one-who-holds-all-power, Christ Jesus. It is God the Son through God the Holy Spirit who enables us to be self-disciplined but only insofar as we yield ourselves to God. Obedience to God and self-discipline through God are repugnant ideas to people who are obsessed with individualism and self-determination.

The irony is that impure motives, unholy attitudes, and addictive behaviors only exist because our human self erroneously thinks that we already have control or that we can have control. Impure motives, unholy attitudes, and addictive behaviors exist because our human self misconcludes that we can control situations, other people, ourselves, and even God when, in truth, we cannot control anything. We indulge a lower, abased, and animal self because it is our way of *trying* to control after learning that we *can never* be in control. We indulge unhealthy and unholy appetites and attitudes because we think magically that we are the ones in control when we indulge them. We indulge them when we seek retaliation and revenge against others, including God. We indulge them whenever we fool ourselves into thinking that we can be in control.

We have never been in control and we shall never be in control; only God is in control. When we think we can be in control, we join ourselves to the ultimate self-deceiver, Satan, who is the eternal Enemy of God. Satan is so self-deceived that he cannot even recognize that he will never have absolute power.

God did not deceive Lucifer. Lucifer deceived Lucifer. Lucifer indulged a self that cannot have real or lasting power. However, the Devil is so far gone emotionally, mentally, and spiritually that he cannot admit that he deceived himself and that he will continue to deceive himself until he is cast into the Lake of Fire at the end of time as we now know it.

Remember, self-discipline does not happen because someone has self-control. Just because we refrain from indulging a lower, abased, or animal self does not mean that we have truly conquered our impure motives, unholy attitudes, and addictive behaviors. True overcoming is done for the glory of God and enabled only by Jesus Christ through God's Holy Spirit. Thus enabled, true overcoming is effortless *(for example,* not requiring personal energy). Overcoming is initiated by Jesus Christ through God's indwelling Holy Spirit and sustained by God for the duration of time that God has appointed it to be sustained (i.e., until we permanently transition to a heavenly plane of consciousness). All control belongs to Jesus Christ. All power belongs to him. God the Son exercises his power in us through the Spirit of God that indwells us. Declarations of truth should only be done after we have sought the Will of God for our lives in every situation and condition and have come to know the mind of God concerning a problematic situation or condition.

Jesus Christ was able to march to his own murder because God's Holy Spirit was on him and resident in him. Likewise, the saved of God through Christ Jesus are only able to endure persecution, tribulation, and suffering because God's Holy Spirit is on them and resident within them. We are only able to do what is contrary to a lower, animal, or abased self — and contrary to a human, conscious functioning, or composite self — through Christ Jesus when we recognize him as our Lord and Savior and when we seek to please him in all that we think, feel, say, and do.

Our human, conscious functioning, or composite self resists the notion that Jesus Christ is the Lord and only Possessor of all power, truth, and control. Jesus Christ is omnipotent. We cannot have power, truth, and control apart from him. There is no power apart from him. Christ Jesus does not hand us power and then detach himself from it or separate himself from us. No, Christ Jesus operates his power through us because those who have accepted him as Savior are not really separate from him. Indeed, we have our one true and only real identity in Christ Jesus. Christ Jesus is our Great I AM — which is to say, our universal Self.

Christ Jesus works through us when we surrender ourselves to him, which occurs when we present ourselves to him in humility and gratitude — without an iota of arrogance. Then, and only then, does he sit fully enthroned within our souls. Until we surrender ourselves to him, the best we can do is offer lip service to him — which, in fact, is really a *dis*service to him (and ourselves).

ego-centrism versus *Ego-centrism*

Throughout this book, the *self* is compared to and contrasted with the *Self.* To avoid possible confusion concerning which one of these two words is being used at any given time, the word *self* (with a lower case "s") never begins a sentence in this book. Instead, *self* is purposely preceded by a conjunction, adjective, adverb, or phrase (just as it is in

19

this sentence) so the reader does not misconclude that *Self* (with an upper case "S") is being discussed.

If this work is ever translated into another language in which there are no upper case letters (*for example*, Chinese, Korean, or Japanese), the present author requests that all of the characters for *Self* (with an upper case "S" in English) be placed within a pair of double angle brackets when writing horizontally (see Table Two in the Appendix for examples) and with the double angle brackets rotated 90 degrees to the right when writing vertically (i.e., with each set of double brackets on its own line).

There is no overlap in the meaning of the words *self* and *Self* when *self* is referring to the lower, animal, or abased self or when *self* is referring to the human, conscious functioning, or composite self. There is, however, overlap in the meaning of the words *self* and *Self* when speaking of one's higher self, supraself, or absolute identity in God. Our higher self, supraself, or absolute identity in God is always in harmony and coincident with our universal Self. Our higher self, supraself, or absolute identity in God is that part of us individually, collectively, and corporately that is one with the Great I AM, our universal Self. Remember, our absolute *Self* is the Great I AM. The Will of the *Self* is also the will of our higher self, supraself, or absolute identity in God. We are completely one with God when our identity coalesces with our universal *Self* and when, concomitantly, God's Will becomes our own will and God's timing becomes our own timing.

In this section, the present author is comparing and contrasting self-centeredness, or ego-centrism, with Self-centeredness, or Ego-centrism. In Latin, the Hebrew expression for "I AM THAT I AM" is most often translated as "EGO SUM QUI SUM." "Ego" is the Latin pronoun for "I" and "sum" is the Latin irregular verb for the first person present tense of "to be." Considering Sigmund Freud's use of "ego" and St. Jerome's use of "Ego" for God's identification of Himself to Moses, it is not outlandish to use the terms "ego-centrism" and "Ego-centrism" as contradistinct to one another.

What does *self-centeredness* mean? The expression *self-centeredness* means that we are petty, arrogant, self-indulgent, controlling, manipulative, prideful, vain, boastful, and self-engrossed. It means that we determine the importance of situations, circumstances, and other people based on whether they impact us favorably or unfavorably (in other words, when we hold the position that others have worth and value only to the degree that we grant them worth and value or to the degree that they validate us). It means that we put ourselves first before others, that we nurse our hurts, that we withhold forgiveness, and that we never do without in order to give to others. By being self-centered, we think of ourselves as more important than God and other people. To be sure, self-centeredness requires that others serve us and feed our massive, wounded egos. Judging or condemning others comes from self-centeredness. So does cruelty.

The truth be told, all that has ever gone wrong with society is based on individual and collective self-centeredness. In a hedonistic society, people especially permit themselves to manifest the qualities and characteristics of an animal, abased, or lower self without remorse and repentance. And they find it so easy to judge and condemn others because they do not stop to think about their own individual insufficiencies, inadequacies, weaknesses, frailties, and vulnerabilities. Even many people who have accepted Christ Jesus as their personal Savior are still left with their own self-centeredness despite their having had a salvation experience. And the almost unending layers of our self-centeredness would put the number of annual rings in a Sequoia or Cedar of Lebanon to shame. Yes, we are rotten almost to the core, but Christ Jesus cleanses us from the inside out. He calls our self-indulgence out to us individually and personally as he asks us to shift our focus away from self-centeredness toward Self-centeredness, which includes the recognition of our one true and only real identity in God, our universal Self.

The Bible articulates what it means to be massively self-centered as it gives a clear overview of the ungodly mindset and actions that result from it:

{29} Being filled with the spirit of unrighteousness, idolatry, wickedness, greed, and evil, egocentric people are full of envy, murder, contentiousness, deceit, and malice for they are slanderers, {30} oppressors, contemptuous of all that is good, exploitive, prideful, vainglorious, inventors of evil things, disobedient to those who look out for their best interests, {31} foolish, faithless, hard-hearted, hostile, unmerciful, {32} who — although knowing the judgment of God (that they which commit such things are worthy of eternal separation from God) — not only do these things but also take pleasure that others think and act similarly.

Romans 1:29-32 KJV Paraphrase

What does it mean to be Self-centered, or Ego-centric? True Self-centeredness, or Ego-centrism, requires us to remember that God is our one true and only real Self and that our absolute identity is actually within the Great I AM. Then, as we shift our focus toward our one true and only real Self, we can see more clearly who we are in and through Christ Jesus. True Self-centeredness permits us to see ourselves in the light of God, which is a spiritual, heavenly, and divine light. When we are Ego-centric, we also see others in that same light for what they are and what they are not. When we are Ego-centric, our lives revolve about God, our universal Self.

In the conscious functioning state in which we now find ourselves, we rarely see ourselves and others in the light of God. For most people, such sight is not a passive process. For most people, seeing ourselves and others in the light of God is an active process. Why is it an active and not a passive process? It is active because it does not come naturally at first; in the beginning, it requires the constant, conscious redirection of our sight from outward appearances to inner realities. Shifting the focus of our composite self — that is, our spirit (personality), our biology (corporeality), our reason (intellect), and our emotion — away from a lower, abased, or animal self toward our higher self, supraself, or absolute identity in God requires personal energy.

Shifting our focus from self to Self requires personal energy because it is a *conscious* redirection. There is a second component in Ego-centrism that does not require energy, but it only develops secondarily. This second component entails surrendering ourselves to God. In our current state of being, the conscious functioning self must step aside and surrender itself in order for the supraself to take over and supernaturally direct, or redirect, our thinking, feeling, attitude, receptivity, expressivity, and action.

Losing Ourselves to Find Our *Self*

Christ Jesus said: "Whoever will save his life shall lose it; and whoever will lose his life for my sake shall find it" (Matthew 16:25 KJV). "Life" here is translated from the Greek ψυχή psü-khā' — which has multiple meanings, including: *soul, life, life force, being, identity,* and *self* — or, in other words, *that which does not dissolve, or cease to exist, at the time of physical death.* At the time of physical death, the natural, or corporeal, body remains earthbound and decomposes but the soul continues on.

Our human self, composite self, or conscious functioning self is weak and fragmented; it does not constitute our whole Self. Only our supraself, or higher self, constitutes our whole Self because it is our absolute identity in the Supraconsciousness of God. We do not begin to find our whole Self until we begin to lose ourselves in God. Because God's Spirit indwells us when we are saved, we have access to who we really are in God through the shed blood of Jesus Christ. God's Holy Spirit, resident within saved souls, permits us access to our one true and only real identity in God, our universal Self. That is why we can only find our Self *within* ourselves; that is why Christ Jesus told us that "the Kingdom of God is *within*" (Luke 17:21 KJV). And that is why the answers to all questions are found *within*.

Christ Jesus also said: "Those who want to follow me should deny themselves and take up their own cross daily" (a combined paraphrase

23

of Matthew 16:24 KJV, Mark 8:34 KJV, and Luke 9:23 KJV). Here, Christ Jesus was speaking of denying the self associated with human instinct and human will.

The Apostle Peter denied three times that he was a follower of Christ Jesus (Matthew 26:34-35). The Apostle Peter allowed his desire for self-survival to take precedence over his desire for Self-survival. Like the Apostle Peter, not only do we deny Christ Jesus in our own verbal expressions but also in our deeds that are idolatrous, disobedient, immoral, unethical, vulgar, and predatory. We must remember that Christ Jesus will deny everyone who denies him in their deeds as well as in their words (Matthew 10:33). To be sure, like the Apostle Peter, we are given time and opportunity to proclaim our love for Christ Jesus by forgiving others, asking God to forgive others, educating others about who Christ Jesus is, and sacrificing ourselves in order to help others gain full realization of God as their universal Self.

In order to lose or deny ourselves, should we commit suicide, elect false martyrdom, or take the blame for the actions of others? No, no, and no! That is not what losing or denying ourselves means. Losing ourselves means losing ourselves in God, whose Will is supreme and sovereign and, therefore, superior to our own individual human wills. In order to deny ourselves, we must choose to enact God's Will in our own lives — even at the expense of our own human *will*.

Being rejected, victimized, and oppressed can play an important role in losing or denying ourselves and finding our one true and only real Self as long as we do not permit ourselves to become bitter, sour, or salty (in the metaphysical sense) about the rejection, victimization, and oppression we experience. (Sometimes, there is power in pain.) We should especially be willing to deny ourselves in order to promote and promulgate the truth even at the expense of our own rejection by well-intentioned family, friends, and colleagues. Personally, the present author has found that speaking out and writing about spiritual truth often causes good people to forsake and desert those who do. Therefore, in order to speak out and write about the truth, one needs to make a conscious decision to do so regardless of the expense to human selfhood and personal relationships.

Our God, Our *Self*

Whomever or whatever we worship, we become. In other words, whom or what we worship eventually becomes our sole identity. If we worship "the god of this world" long enough (2 Corinthians 4:4 KJV), then our identity is eternally lost in and absorbed by the identity of that god. If we worship our human self, then we turn ourselves over to a false identity. If we worship the Lord God Almighty with all of our heart, soul, strength, and mind, then our identity becomes completely, fully, perfectly, and eternally absorbed in Him.

We become whomever or whatever we worship because we are fused to whom or what we worship and are infused by the identity of whom or what we worship as well. Rather than proclaim that Jesus Christ is our first priority because we worship him and him alone, we need to recognize that there is no such thing as priority when every aspect of our being is permeated by Jesus Christ. The question of priority is moot when we have turned ourselves over to our Creator-God.

In this world, we can be separated from whom or what we worship only by choice because we alone choose whom or what we worship. Thus, just as we can choose salvation and deliverance by accepting Christ Jesus as our personal Savior, so can we also throw salvation and deliverance away in order to worship a false self-identity.

We worship what we desire and desire what we worship; and we worship what we love and love what we worship. Since we worship what we love and desire, does that mean that God worships us? No, although we are the "apple of God's eye," or the "object of His desire," God does not worship us. Although God commends us for thinking, feeling, speaking, and doing the right thing, God does not praise us as an object of worship. Although God adores us as His created, God does not worship us. God as our universal Self, and as Creator of all that is, deserves to be worshiped. We do not. "It is God who has created us and not we ourselves" (Psalm 100:3b KJV Paraphrase). When God created us, God elected us — individually, collectively, and corporately — to be His companion, not His Creator. He alone is Creator. We are created beings, never the Creator. The Creator alone deserves to be worshiped.

When do human beings seek to be worshiped? We seek to be worshiped: (1) whenever we place ourselves on a pedestal above others; (2) whenever we try to impress others with how witty and capable we are; and (3) whenever we boast of the gifts, talents, and blessings that God has given to us as if we deserved them. We worship ourselves whenever we refuse to die daily in the Name of our Lord Jesus Christ. We worship ourselves, and seek for others to worship us as well, whenever we seek infamy, notoriety, or celebrity for the sake of proclaiming our own name and advancing our own reputation rather than proclaiming the name and advancing the reputation of Jesus Christ.

Healing Metaphysically

We intercede metaphysically for those in need by appealing to the higher self, supraself, or absolute identity of the individual we are prayerfully treating. We appeal to that self by entreating it — or attempting to awaken it — in the individual we are treating by declaring, proclaiming, and affirming spiritual, supernatural, and metaphysical truths that are Biblically-based on behalf of the person receiving treatment (even if we are that person) or by having the individual we are treating declare, proclaim, and affirm for themselves spiritual, supernatural, and metaphysical truths that are Biblically-based by repeating the declarations, proclamations, and affirmations we identify and generate for them to repeat.

In order to successfully treat those in need, we must forgo complacency. We must refuse to yield to a false image of ourselves or an untrue self-identity. We must rise spiritually to every occasion.

Should we be disappointed, embarrassed, or angry if a metaphysically treated condition does not respond favorably to treatment? No. Being disappointed, embarrassed, and angry are signs that we desire to be in control rather than desiring for God to be in control; they are also signs that we do not trust God enough to let Him be in control. We seek to wrest control from God, but, of course, that is not possible. We must remember that God's Will is not our own will and that God's timing is not our own timing. And we must remember that God's definition of healing is often quite different from our own.

What is a *Christian metaphysician*? A *Christian metaphysician* is a spiritual light-bearer. What makes someone a *spiritual light-bearer?* A spiritual light-bearer carries spiritual light to any given situation through the messages of truth, hope, and understanding that he or she brings. Because Christ Jesus is spiritual Light, or *light-in-itself,* a spiritual light-bearer carries the presence of Christ Jesus to cancel the power of spiritual darkness in any difficult situation. Not only do Satan, all fallen angels, and all unclean spirits have no love of spiritual light, they are afraid of spiritual light. That is why they inhabit spiritual darkness. Consequently, Satan, all fallen angels, and all unclean spirits will always shrink away from messages of truth, hope, and understanding. Christian metaphysicians use this knowledge to combat the fear and anxiety that evil seeks to induce through its lies and intimidation. A Christian metaphysician acknowledges the existence of evil at the same time that he or she is confident of evil's ultimate demise, defeat, and destruction.

If someone that you know suffers from fear, anxiety, despair, despondency, or depression, then bring them a message for both today and tomorrow: a message of spiritual truth that will help them metaphysically understand their predicament as well as help them have hope. It is advisable that you acknowledge the presence of something negative in someone else's life *only* if you leave the person with a message of truth, hope, and understanding. If you cannot think of a specific message of truth, hope, and understanding to say, then read aloud to that person a message of truth, hope, and understanding from the Holy Bible. Teach this tactic to others in order for them to fight Satan's mortal mind. During the Millennium of Peace, when Satan's mortal mind will be bound, this tactic will also prove useful in helping people to override negative emotions induced by their own individual carnal mind (i.e., fleshly mind).

Exercises and Activities in Christian Metaphysics

1. What did Christ Jesus mean when he said: "I AM"? How does this statement relate to God as our *Self?*

2. How are obedience and disobedience to God's Will related to the spiritual evolution of created beings?

3. What does it mean to use the Name of God in vain?

4. Why is it best not to use the name *Jesus* alone or the word *Christ* alone?

5. What is required to understand the triadic nature of God?

6. What is the difference between *self* and *Self?*

7. What does the *self* include for each fallen created being in corporeality?

8. In what way or ways can fallen created beings apprehend metaphysical reality?

9. Compare and contrast the meaning of the words *eternal* and *immortal* as used in this book.

10. From which perspective is spiritual, supernatural, or metaphysical reality knowable?

11. Are all emotions negative? Why or why not?

12. What does the infilling of God's Holy Spirit presage?

13. List the correct sequence for the following events: "a new heaven and a new earth," World War IV (the Battle of Gog and Magog), the return of Jesus Christ to Earth, and the Great White Throne Judgment.

14. To what is the phrase *"life after life after death"* referring?

15. What four elements comprise the human, conscious functioning, or composite self?

16. Why do human beings have faulty and unstable emotions?

17. What does the statement "God is our universal Self" mean to you?

18. Why is it detrimental to deny or ignore that you have a lower, animal, or abased self?

19. How are natural consequences used by God to help discipline us?

20. Are people who belong to God separate from one another? Why or why not?

21. Briefly discuss saved created beings in relation to the power of Christ Jesus.

22. How much personal credit should we take for recognizing absolute truth or for having a glimpse of the truth?

23. Can you discover absolute truth for another person? Why or why not?

24. In what way is self-discovery not a spiritual reality?

25. Is God's grace and mercy predictable? Why or why not?

26. Is obtaining God's grace and mercy formulaic? Why or why not?

27. What does it mean to proclaim that you are whole?

28. In God's spiritual reality, who has all power and control?

29. Briefly describe the importance of obedience to God and self-discipline through God to your own life.

30. What constraints are placed on declarations of faith?

31. Is there ever overlap in the meaning of the words *self* and *Self*? Please explain.

32. What are the major differences between self-centeredness and Self-centeredness?

33. How is energy required for seeing ourselves and others in the light of God?

34. How do we lose or deny ourselves?

35. Should we exalt self or Self? Please explain.

36. When do human beings seek to be worshiped?

37. In your own words, explain how we intercede for others metaphysically.

38. How does the definition of healing differ between God and most human beings?

39. What is a *Christian metaphysician?*

Chapter Two

Preparing to Meet Our *Self*

Being Who We Really Are

We can meet our one true and only real self (i.e., who we are in God, our universal Self) only where God dwells. In Old Testament times, one could meet one's universal Self only on holy ground: (1) like the Prophet Moses on Mount Sinai, or (2) like the High Priest in the Holy of Holies in the Exodus Tabernacle or Jerusalem Temple. During these New Testament times, however, authentic believers in Christ Jesus have free access to their universal Self through the shed blood of Jesus Christ, which blood has dissolved the temporal barrier between God and human beings who are saved. For each saved human being, the house of the Lord today is the tabernacle, or physical body, that is cohabited by both the individual soul and the Spirit of God. (For a saved person still in corporeality, the Holy Spirit indwells the soul and the soul inhabits the physical body.) Saved souls meet God, their universal Self, in the Holy of Holies — metaphysically represented by the cranium, wherein dwells the Supraconsciousness of God through His Holy Spirit.[7]

Although saved souls have *free* access to the Supraconsciousness of God, it is not cheap and easy access. It comes with a personal price. Just as Moses had to remove his shoes before he stepped onto holy ground in front of the burning bush (Exodus 3:2), and just as the High Priest had to prepare himself emotionally, mentally, physically, and

---

[7] Read the chapters on the Skeletal System and Nervous System in *Divine Metaphysics of Human Anatomy* by Joseph Adam Pearson, ISBN 978-0985772819.

spiritually before he entered the Holy of Holies to commune with God, so also do saved people need to prepare themselves to meet God, their universal Self, and commune most intimately with Him. As Jacob's fight at Peniel proved (Genesis 32:24-30), it is always a struggle to meet God face-to-face; we need to be willing to fight against worldly, fleshly, and unclean desires.

So, how do we prepare to meet God, our universal Self, and commune with Him? We prepare by living holy lives. How do we live holy lives? We live holy lives: (1) by praying to God, thinking holy thoughts, feeling holy emotions, speaking in holy ways, and doing holy things; and (2) by praying to God, eschewing unholy thoughts, redirecting our focus away from unholy emotions, refraining from speaking in unholy ways, and resisting actions and behaviors that are unholy.

During Old Testament times, especially before the Babylonian Captivity (598/597 – 538 BCE), the children of Israel often departed from worshiping God, going as far as incorporating idolatrous objects and practices into activities within the Jerusalem Temple. So, too, do those of us who claim to be saved often bring idolatrous objects and vulgar practices into our own bodies by entertaining unclean thoughts, feelings, ideas, and images. Too often, we do not prepare on a daily basis to meet God as our universal Self. We do not take stock of ourselves. We do not assess ourselves. It is easier to take stock of others and assess them instead. It is easier to avoid evaluating our own weaknesses, frailties, and vulnerabilities and evaluate someone else's.

A recurring theme in this book is that we must be obedient to God's Will and discipline ourselves in the power of God's Holy Spirit through the shed blood of Jesus Christ. Obedience and discipline are required for us to be who we really are in God, our universal Self.

The Holy and the Vulgar

Although the most obvious antonym for *holy* is *unholy,* nuances for the word *unholy* are often blithely overlooked by many people, especially authentic Christians who live in materialistic, self-centered, and self-indulgent societies. For that reason, I will now transition to using the word *vulgar* instead of *unholy* as the antonym for *holy.*

Vulgar, as used in this work, means "crude, primitive, self-abasing, self-loathing, materialistic, self-centered, self-indulgent, covetous, lustful, and animal-like." To be vulgar means that one entertains thoughts, feelings, ideas, and images that are *abuse-oriented, addiction-driven,* and/or *sexually-indulgent.* Of course, there is often an overlap in these three categories because the majority of human beings are poly-abusers, poly-addicts, and poly-indulgers. Unless vulgar thoughts, feelings, ideas, and imagined images are instantly and constantly placed under the feet of Jesus Christ, they control us and eventually play out in multiple ways not only in our imaginations but also in our daily behaviors.

Abuse-oriented, addiction-driven, and *sexually-indulgent* thoughts, feelings, ideas, images, and behaviors are harmful to us, our families and friends, and societies throughout the world. They indulge our own carnal mind as well as Satan's mortal mind. They are harmful to us because they reduce us to predatory beasts. They are harmful to others because they reduce them to objects of prey for self-gratification. *Abuse-oriented* people want positions of power so they can control, manipulate, and exploit others (even if it is only in a supervisory role over people in menial positions); they desire to control the thoughts, emotions, belief systems, and actions of others. *Addiction-driven* people reduce themselves metaphysically to lizards, rats, hyenas, snakes, and vultures that perpetually seek to avoid discomfort as well as be maximally insulated from the difficulties of human life. *Sexually-indulgent* people like to listen to as well as articulate foul language that induces lustful and even violent thoughts, feelings, ideas, images, and behaviors in themselves and in others; they like to imagine, dream about, view, and/or perform sexual acts that induce and attempt to satiate the basest desires of their own animality. They don't realize that, in their imaginations and dreams, they are having sex with unclean spirits, demons, and devils (remember, all three terms are used synonymously in this work as well as within the various translations of the Holy Bible).

The Strange Case of Dr. Jekyll and Mr. Hyde, an 1886 novella by Robert Louis Stevenson, graphically depicts an extreme case of dissociative identity disorder that represents good and evil personalities co-existing within every human being. The *Island of Dr. Moreau,* an 1896 novel by H. G. Wells, depicts human-like beings who regress to their original animal state to feed from the flesh and blood of killed animals. *Dracula,* an 1897 novel by Bram Stoker, depicts the *undead* who feed by drinking blood from living creatures, sucking their very life from them. A plethora of other books and various media depict creatures with reanimated flesh, the *walking dead,* or zombies who feed off of living human flesh — often with a penchant for devouring human brains.

All media in the genre of nightmarish and ghoulish horror play upon the notion that human beings revert to predatory animal instincts by indulging their own carnal mind and Satan's mortal mind. To be sure, this genre is archetypal and quintessential of the created spiritual being who spoils himself/herself by yielding to temptations associated with vulgarity. Overall, the beings depicted in this genre represent the descent into depravity of the created spirit of a once unfallen and pristine being who mentally, emotionally, and spiritually *snaps* by entering into temptation and then is ever prone to continuously fall even farther from the Creator-God as its soul spirals downward until it finally becomes a devil, demon, or unclean spirit itself.

Entering into Temptation

First and foremost, temptation is a substate, or substratum, of Satan's mortal mind and, although not exclusively so, a condition of being human. Although temptation may be a state without a place, it is never a place without a state. Without regard to geographic position or locality, we enter into temptation whenever we entertain self-centered and errant thoughts, feelings, ideas, and images. Indulging them eventually causes us to *realize* them in our behaviors and, in this way, they become our reality.

Simply stated, human beings are prone to sin. The instant we announce that we have conquered temptations concerning a particular area or arena in our life is the exact moment that we enter into temptation and set ourselves up to sin. Unfortunately, sin is like an itch; once you scratch it, it wants continued scratching. (Although the original quote that the present author heard from a classmate in his high school gym locker room was "*sex* is like an itch ...," he has broadened it to "*sin* is like an itch ..." because of its relevance here.)

The greatest problem with the "Word-of-faith" religious movement, like so many other religious movements, is that its devotees are not permitted to think or say: "The problem with the Word-of-faith movement is..." Declaring God's goodness, proclaiming the truth, and laying claim to who we are in God are positive things but only when we permit ourselves critical analysis and dissent in agreeable disagreement with others. Our supraself cannot take over if we deny that our sin nature exists or if we misconclude that our individual will supplants the Will of God. Yes, we can deny control to our lower, animal, or abased self but not by pretending that it does not exist. How can we take a bull by the horns if we pretend there is no bull?

Errant, self-centered desire opens the door to temptation. Continuing in such desire causes us to walk through the door to enter a full-fledged state of temptation. Unfortunately, the door to temptation does not just lead to one temptation but temptations of many kinds.

That is why most human beings are poly-abusers, poly-addicts, and poly-indulgers. As soon as we enter temptation, we are flooded with thoughts, feelings, ideas, and images that relate to many different kinds of temptation all at the same time. In temptation, we are in a personally weakened state and, therefore, not easily able to resist tugs and pulls for us to do things that are dishonoring to ourselves and others as well as dishonoring to God.

In order to not open the door to temptation, we must quell any and all desire to do anything that is displeasing to God and potentially harmful to ourselves or others. We quell desire by praying to God, thinking the thoughts of God, reading the Holy Bible out loud, and silently meditating on the truths and principles found in God's written Word.

Once we enter into a state of temptation, it is very difficult to exit. However, prayer can return us to a state outside of temptation. That is why praying for ourselves and for others to be returned from a state of temptation is not only important but necessary.

Before Christ Jesus returns to rule from Earth during the Millennium of Peace, entering a state of temptation is compounded by Satan's mortal mind, which exists not only within Satan but also in his fallen angels and unclean spirits (unclean spirits are the discarnate souls of those who have permanently rejected Christ Jesus and, thus, are eternally outside the Will of God). Once Christ Jesus returns to Earth, Satan's mortal mind will be bound for one thousand years. Then, although Satan's mortal mind will be unable to influence human beings, human beings will still be influenced negatively by their own carnal minds, corporeal natures, and worldly desires.

At the time that Christ Jesus returns to Earth, the souls of all authentic Christians, living as well as dead, will receive their redeemed bodies, or renewed somatic identities. As joint-heirs with Jesus Christ, they will not be tempted to sin because they will not be in corruptible bodies; thus, they will not have vulnerabilities, frailties, or infirmities. All other souls who remain in physical flesh will continue to be

tempted by their own carnal minds because they are in corporeality —
even though Satan and his potential to influence will be bound for one
thousand years.

Those of you who are reading this during the Millennium of Peace
(i.e., while Christ Jesus is ruling the universe from the planet Earth)
need to stand fast against errant thoughts, feelings, ideas, and images
that are products of your own carnal minds or you will end up
standing with Satan in the final battle between good and evil at the
end of the Millennium of Peace — during World War IV, which is
referred to as the battle of "Gog and Magog" in Revelation 20:7-10.[8]

All people in physical flesh are tempted, first and foremost, through
the desires of their own carnal minds. Carnal thoughts of abuse,
addiction, and indulgence form in our imaginations. (Our
imaginations serve as projection screens for fantasized thinking.)
Vain, vulgar, and violent thoughts are usually more easily controlled
when they are fantasized during our waking hours as daydreams. In
contrast, unless we are hypervigilant during sleep, such fantasized
thoughts more easily overtake our subconscious, or unconscious,
thoughts to steer us in the direction of walking through the door of
temptation. When they are unleashed and unchecked, vain, vulgar,
and violent fantasized thinking fulfills self-centered and errant desires
of abuse, addiction, and indulgence by causing us to act out sinfully
during sleep. Always pervasive within Satan's realm (i.e., within him,
within his fallen angels, and within his unclean spirits), Satan's mortal
mind can trigger thoughts, feelings, ideas, and images in our own
carnal minds and augment them to possess our subconscious, or
unconscious, thinking because carnality itself is inherent in each
person in the corporeal, or incarnate, state. To be sure, our own
carnality can trigger vain, vulgar, and violent fantasized thinking

---

[8] Just as "Babylon" in the Holy Bible has different specific meanings in the Old and New
Testaments (for example, in 2 Kings, 2 Chronicles, Ezra, Nehemiah, Esther, Psalms,
Isaiah, Jeremiah, Ezekiel, Daniel, Micah, and Zechariah versus 1 Peter 5:13 and
Revelation 14:8; 16:19; 17:5; and 18:2, 10, & 21), so do "Gog and Magog" have different
specific meanings in the Old and New Testaments (for example, in Ezekiel 38:2 versus
Revelation 20:8).

independent of Satan's mortal mind. That is why temptation will still exist for those in physical flesh during the Millennium of Peace. (If it did not exist, there would be no joining of evil spiritual forces to provide a platform for World War IV at the end of the Millennium of Peace.)

Beside Our *Self*

Without the Presence of God's Holy Spirit indwelling us, human beings are no better than beasts of burden or brute beasts. When they fit into the category of beasts of burden, human beings live, labor, and toil in vain. If brute beasts, human beings act like feral animals — *for example,* as thieves, murderers, bullies, terrorists, sexual predators, and con artists. Regardless of how charming, cultured, and ingratiating human beings might seem, as beasts of burden they wear a facade with no substance behind it. And, regardless of how intimidating human beings might seem, as brute beasts they have no real or lasting power.

Without God as our universal Self, we are beside our Self and cannot fulfill the destiny that God has for us. Without God as our universal Self, we miss the mark and are not even close to the target. Without the Spirit of God abiding within us, or without our allowing that Spirit to have absolute sway over us, we are not able to resist temptation. In fact, without the Spirit of God, we do not even recognize what temptation is.

Without the Spirit of God indwelling them through the shed blood of Jesus Christ, human beings remain ignorant, stupid, foolish, and even wicked — regardless of how well-educated, cultured, and polite they are.

When Satan becomes our *self*

Satan is not just a force. Satan is an entity with consciousness and volition. In this book, Satan's evil consciousness is often referred to as *mortal mind*. To emphasize that such an evil consciousness belongs to a clever being with free will, the present author thinks it important to use the noun phrase "Satan's mortal mind" when referring to that being's pervasive intellect, cunning, and willfulness. The problem with just using the phrase "mortal mind" alone is that readers and hearers often conclude that mortal mind is a nebulous force, like gravity, and cannot be met head-on or does not need to be confronted face-to-face. Without the possessive form of "Satan" as the qualifier, the phrase "mortal mind" has the same problems as the phrase "divine Mind" when that nomenclature is used as an appellation for God. To resolve controversy and clarify them both, it is best to regularly (although not necessarily always) explicitly state that it is "Satan's mortal mind" or that it is "God's divine Mind" about which we are thinking, speaking, or writing.

Without God as our universal Self or Satan as our chosen self-identity, we are left to a human, conscious functioning, and composite self that is totally defined by its designated and/or assumed societal roles — *for example,* as parent, spouse, child, employer, employee, benefactor, recipient, leader, or follower. To be sure, we can fulfill multiple societal roles at the same time. And we can fulfill societal roles without God as our universal Self or without Satan as our chosen self-identity, but not for long. The present author writes "but not for long" because, sooner or later, we become united with one or the other by becoming who and what we worship, honor, venerate, and love. Eventually, we choose who we are by yielding to God or submitting to Satan.

Judas Iscariot, the one-time Apostle of Jesus Christ, is an excellent example of someone for whom Satan became his *self.* As fiscal agent for the first group of Christian disciples, he fit well into his societal role of treasurer and accountant. His personality was one that permitted him to think in terms of black and white, credits and debits, and addition and subtraction. Judas was impressed by his own abilities to think in clever and calculating ways. Judas also fooled himself into thinking that he was benevolent at the same time that he thought he had all of the answers. Actually, Judas often functioned from the standpoint of his own carnal mind, which is the intellect of the lower, abased, or animal self.[9] Because Judas was already pointed in the direction of extreme selfishness and willfulness, Satan was able to enter into him through the portal that Judas himself had created and opened. That Judas was smart and religious did not keep him from being used as Satan's tool. Had Judas really believed Jesus Christ to be the *only-begotten* Son of God, he would have not only experienced remorse for his crime against God but also demonstrated true repentance by going to God in prayer, confessing his sin, and asking God for forgiveness. Instead, Judas remained the "son of perdition" (John 17:12 KJV) and child of hell that he purposed himself to be. Judas died in his sins (i.e., without repenting of them and having them forgiven).

What happened to Judas is representative of what happens to all who permit themselves to be used by Satan's mortal mind. They are not given a special place of honor by Satan. They are left by Satan to their own torment and to fend for themselves. Satan never cares for his pawns and puppets — not at the onset of using them, not while he is using them, and not after he is done with them. Expect nothing from Satan. Remember, Satan is a liar and the father of all lies. Satan's promises are empty and only filled with his own derisive laughter.

Our One True and Only Real Enemy

Satan's mortal mind encroaches on our personal space whenever we give it the opportunity. We give Satan's mortal mind an opportunity to

---

[9] It is important to emphasize here that the *animal self* is not just a "brute beast" but also a brain-based neurological creature whose thinking can be cunning, crafty, clever, and refined at the same time that it is ungodly.

broadcast unwholesome and unclean messages to the radio receiver of our mind: (1) whenever we do not trust the Lord completely (i.e., whenever we distrust Him); (2) whenever we are jealous of another person or envious of what that person has; (3) whenever we lust after (i.e., strongly desire) what we ought not to desire; (4) whenever we withhold forgiveness from another person; and (5) whenever we become bitter about circumstances beyond our control.

(1) Distrust

When we do not trust in the Lord completely to cause "all things to come together for good for those who love Him and are the called according to His purpose" (Romans 8:28 KJV Paraphrase), we open a metaphysical portal for Satan's intrusive mortal mind. Not trusting in the Lord completely is the same as doubting that the Lord can do the impossible for one person or for all of humanity — providing, of course, that the so-called impossible is not inconsistent or contradictory to God's Nature.

Although it may sound extreme, not trusting in the Lord is equivalent to doubting that the Lord exists. And doubting that the Lord exists metaphysically ties His hands when it comes to His answering our prayers and rewarding us: Scripture states plainly that "in order to please God, the person who approaches Him must believe that He exists and that He rewards those who diligently seek Him" (Hebrews 11:6 KJV Paraphrase). It is we who falter in our faith in God and not God in His faithfulness to us.

When we are uncertain about God's love and care for us or uncertain about His interest and involvement in our daily lives, we worry, have anxiety, and experience doubt because we let Satan begin to fill us with his spirit of fear. Satan's spirit of fear is the antithesis of God's Spirit of love, comfort, peace, and truth. Satan's mortal mind, *a vampiric semi-consciousness,* speaks lies to us on the broadband wavelength of his spirit of fear, inviting us to hurt others, hurt ourselves, and attempt to hurt God.

Trusting the Lord completely is way beyond being optimistic or refraining from being negative. Trusting the Lord completely includes viewing each challenge as an additional opportunity to praise the Lord for His protection and His impeccable timing for the particular challenge at hand and the circumstances surrounding it as well as its promised resolution. We need to look for the opportunities for good in every challenge and remember that God has not given to us more than we can bear or carry (1 Corinthians 10:13).

Whenever we sense Satan's spirit of fear invading us, we must spontaneously seek to regain our footing of faith in God by returning all of our trust to Him by: (1) praying, (2) meditating on His written Word, and (3) declaring that Jesus Christ possesses all power in Heaven and on Earth.

We are not to place our trust in human beings, situations, or our own abilities; we are to place all trust in Jesus Christ, and Jesus Christ alone. To be sure, there is a delicate balance between relying radically on God to meet all of our needs and seeking for God's Will to be done. Yes, God meets our every need but not always in ways that we expect or in ways that we think He should. Yes, God's divine love is unfaltering and unwavering, but God's divine love ministers to our spiritual needs first. Our spiritual needs often do not match our physical needs.

Although it may be nice to receive comfort and encouragement from another human being, we are not to rely on receiving such support. Instead, we are to expect and seek comfort and encouragement from God's Holy Spirit. God is who He says He is. It is God's Holy Spirit that is our Comforter and Encourager. (Of course, God's Holy Spirit can, and does, work through others to comfort and encourage us.)

When we have chronic pain — or, for that matter, any other unrelenting problem — that does not respond favorably to medical, spiritual, or mechanical means of treatment, there is usually a spiritual reason for the recurring pain or continuing problem. The pain or problem may serve as a regulator, or metaphysical *thorn*, that keeps us from sinning or returning to the same sin that was the primary cause of the pain or problem. The pain or problem may also serve as a test of our faithfulness to God and a testimony of His faithfulness to us. Metaphysically speaking, problems beget problems that teach us lessons: (1) about our deficiencies, weaknesses, flaws, and vulnerabilities; and (2) about the immensity of God's goodness and love for us.

Doubting God's ability to provide for us, reward us, bless us, and resolve our problems is no less spiritual idolatry than believing in doctrinal error that is heresy or apostasy. We are heretics and apostates when we believe that some obstacles are too big to be removed from us by God or that some problems and challenges are too great to be resolved by Him. This includes obstacles and problems that are temporal as well as those that are spiritual.

(2) Jealousy and Envy

Jealousy refers to a feeling that one person has about another person or group of people that is borne of possessiveness, or a false sense of ownership, privilege, and entitlement. Created beings cannot — nor should they try to — possess other human beings, regardless of relationship. Spousal, friend, and business relationships do not entitle anyone to own anyone else or to rule, manipulate, or exploit the thoughts, feelings, and actions of others. When created beings seek to be in a master-slave relationship with any other created being, they consciously or unconsciously seek to be that person's *self*, identity, and god; in other words, the so-called *possessor* seeks to be loved, worshiped, and obeyed by the so-called *possessed*. In effect, the jealous person seeks to replace the Lord God Almighty for the possessed person and become that person's god. Ironically, the person who seeks to be in bondage to another person desires to worship someone other than the Creator. To be sure, any bondage-domination relationship is a match made in hell.

The only entity in the universe who is justifiably jealous is the Creator-God. The Creator-God is justifiably jealous for the love and affection of His errant created beings, who have consciously or unconsciously given their love and affection to another (i.e., Satan).

Envy refers to feelings that one person has concerning the things, characteristics, skills, and traits that another person or group of people actually possesses or is thought to possess.

(3) Lust

Lust is the ungodly, unholy, and unhealthy desire for the things of this world. Sexual lust glorifies the animal, lower, or abased *self* and reduces others to pawns, puppets, and objects for self-gratification. Sexual lust — as well as lust for riches, power, and position — causes us to compromise, disregard, or abandon our spiritual ideals or our quest for them.

The human carnal mind and Satan's mortal mind intersect best at the level of lust. First, we are tempted by the impure desires associated with our own carnal mind; then, Satan's mortal mind tempts us more powerfully by magnifying our perception of the pleasurable outcomes we would experience if we indulged those desires. Our own lust opens the door to enhanced enticement from Satan's mortal mind. Lust of the human carnal mind elaborates (i.e., constructs) a projection screen upon which Satan's mortal mind casts its unreal images and illusions to build unwholesome scenarios that play out in our imaginations. When we misconclude that the images, illusions, and scenarios are real and justify to ourselves that it is alright for us to act on temptations associated with them, they *do* become real for us and we become entangled in their web through our actions, which actions are ultimately based on the impure desires of our heart.
The only good thing about temptation is that it points out to us our own individual weaknesses, frailties, and vulnerabilities as well as where and when we should shore up our faith in God, our universal Self.

(4) Unforgiveness

Like lust, unforgiveness is a condition of the heart. The lower, animal, or abased self does not have the capacity to forgive but it does have the capacity to withhold forgiveness. The lower, animal, or abased self either runs away from a source of unpleasantness or seeks to destroy it. The human, conscious functioning, or composite self also does not have the capacity to forgive, but it can fool itself into thinking that it does (the human self cannot forgive but its vengeance can be appeased). Similar to the lower self, the human self can withhold forgiveness and nurse hurts. It is only the higher *self*, supraself, or absolute identity we have in God that has the capacity to forgive. Unlike the lower self and the human self, the higher self does not have the capacity to withhold forgiveness.

When God is our universal Self, we forgive others without hesitation. Translating forgiveness to the human experience becomes natural for us when we allow our supraself to override our conscious functioning self.

(5) Bitterness

Bitterness comes when we nurse and rehearse actual hurts as well as perceived wrongs against us. Bitterness usually accompanies unforgiveness, especially when unforgiveness has become a way of life. Bitterness is a poison that spoils inner peace, our relationships with others, and what we are able to accomplish while we are on Earth. When people do not repent of their bitterness and actions based on it, they eventually perish in their own corruption; indeed, they become no better than brute beasts. These feral animals are the wandering stars "to whom is reserved the blackness of darkness throughout all eternity" (Jude, Verse 13 KJV). At this juncture, the present author recommends that the reader pause and review both the Epistle of Jude and Chapter Two of the Second Epistle of Peter in the Holy Bible.

The Portal to a Hellish State of Existence

Before we transition completely and permanently from this earth plane of consciousness to the Kingdom of God (i.e., a heavenly plane of consciousness), God wants us to surrender all things, ideas, practices, and indulgences that are displeasing to Him. He wants us to always choose pleasing Him over pleasing our human selves, our carnal selves, or Satan's mortal mind. God wants us to freely renounce every iota of vulgarity and violence in our lives at the same time that we remember not to judge people who continue to be vulgar and violent (we may keep our distance from them and make accurate observations about them, but we are not to judge them).

When each one of us is tempted to do that which is displeasing to God (i.e., not in synch with God's Will for us), we are presented with a metaphysical doorknob that we may turn or refrain from turning. The doorknob is part of the door, or portal, to a hellish state of existence. To be sure, hell is a place, but hell is also a state of existence. Hell is a place where God is *not*. We enter a hellish state of existence when we consciously choose to turn that doorknob (i.e., take Satan's bait), open the door, and enter into temptation.

From a practical standpoint, we willfully enter into temptation, *for example:* (1) when, without spiritual preparation, we read something that we know will provoke us to get angry or be depressed; (2) when we knowingly open a magazine or web page that will evoke thoughts and feelings of sexual lust; (3) when we enter a casino if it has been impossible in the past for us to stop gambling while there; or (4) when we enter a bar or tavern if we are in a tenuous recovery from alcohol abuse.

God does not want us to willfully enter into temptation. Entering into temptation includes mentally, emotionally, spiritually, and sometimes physically going where we ought not to go. If we go where we ought not to go, we demonstrate that we are not spiritually mature enough to discipline ourselves. Unless we demonstrate that we are mature enough to discipline ourselves, God will not entrust us with tasks (or additional tasks) that fulfill His purpose for us and our destiny in Him.

How do we discipline ourselves and, thereby, keep ourselves from entering into temptation? By praying continuously to God that He keep us from willfully entering into temptation. We must nip sin at the level of its bud, temptation. Only God through His Holy Spirit has the power to keep us from temptation. God does not lead us into temptation. Without praying unceasingly to God, we will act on our own and through our own power. And our own power is insufficient to keep us from willfully entering into temptation. It is only God's power that can keep us from yielding to temptation. That is why we must pray, and we must pray continuously.

It is God's greatest gift to us when He gives us tasks that fulfill His purpose. Paradoxically, completing those tasks not only fulfills His purpose, it fulfills our destiny in Him — the destiny He has created for us individually, collectively, and corporately. Willfully entering into temptation keeps us from fulfilling our destiny in God. It keeps us from doing what God would have us do for His glory.

During sleep, sleep deprivation, and general fatigue, human beings are more vulnerable to temptation. Our spiritual defenses are down during such times. While we are asleep, and when we are sleep-deprived or fatigued, thoughts and images from our carnal mind redirect our focus away from pleasing God toward pleasing our fleshly mind and earthly body. At the same time, thoughts and images from Satan's mortal mind fan the flames of such inclinations toward full-blown disobedience by inserting themselves within our subconscious, or unconscious, mind, tugging us in the direction of Satan's hellish state of existence. Because Satan is a worm and the portal to his enblackened consciousness is a wormhole, we continue to be pulled in the direction of his nothingness when we willfully enter into a state of temptation.

However, no state of temptation is so great that it can prevent us from exiting it even after we have willingly entered into it. Why? Jesus

Christ is not only "the Door" and "the Way" to an intimate relationship with God, Jesus Christ also provides "the Exit" out of a hellish state of existence when we metaphysically apply his shed blood to the circumstances (i.e., images and illusions) of the temptation at hand. It is through the application of the shed blood of Jesus Christ that the images and illusions of temptation dissipate and disappear. Visualizing and applying the shed blood of Jesus Christ to unclean desires and false images and illusions provide an excellent example of using Christian metaphysics in a most practical way.

Although God continues to offer His mercy to us, God feels no pity for us when we willingly enter into a state of temptation. Instead, God asks us these questions: (1) "Did you ask Me to keep you from entering into temptation?" (2) "Did you ask Me for strength to resist Satan's mortal mind?" And (3) "Are you using *the Exit* that I provided for you through Jesus Christ?"

God expects us to use what He has provided in order for us to return to His redemptive state of consciousness — which is to say, the state of mind we have in Christ Jesus.

In summary, expect to discipline your thoughts and actions only by the power of Christ Jesus through God's Holy Spirit. Pray to God to keep you from entering into temptation. Pray to God for His strength to resist the Devil. And if you find yourself already in a hellish state of existence because you have willingly entered into temptation, rouse yourself by metaphysically applying the shed blood of Jesus Christ to the false images and illusions associated with the temptation.

Always remember, in addition to being *the Door* and *the Way,* Christ Jesus also remains *the Exit* from a hellish state of existence. For this reason, it should now be apparent that one does not walk out of temptation the same way that one entered it.

Before God came to Earth as *God the Son,* or *God in flesh,* God did not know experientially what temptation is. God did not know because God had never experienced temptation for Himself before. It may sound strange to read, and it is certainly strange for the present author to write, but, before His incarnation as Jesus Christ, the Creator-God only had an academic knowledge of temptation. Because God is omniscient, He knew what temptation is and could have written a highly precise 100,000 volume encyclopedia about it, but He had never before experienced it for Himself. This understanding helps to resolve the seeming dilemma concerning the Biblical truth that, although "God cannot be tempted with evil" (James 1:13b KJV), God the Son "was in all points tempted like as *we are*" (Hebrews 4:15b KJV).

There are two reasons that the Godhead came to Earth as God the Son: (1) The first reason was to save us from our iniquity and sin by providing the only acceptable substitutionary blood atonement, or offering, for the remission, or cancellation, of our sins (through the crucifixion of Jesus Christ). (2) And the second reason was for God Himself to experience what temptation is so that "He could be touched with the feeling of our infirmities" (Hebrews 4:15a KJV) — in order that His mercy would continually flow to those of us still in corporeality who sin, repent, repeat the same sin again, and then repent again, over and over and over. (This describes all saved human beings: None of us are without sin or without the propensity to sin.) Because "the fullness of the Godhead indwelt Christ Jesus bodily" (Colossians 2:9 KJV Paraphrase), the entire Godhead now knows experientially (i.e., personally, intimately, and practically) how heinous temptation really is. The intersection of this experiential understanding with the blood sacrifice of Christ Jesus even created a portal for Christ Jesus to visit souls in Hades (Acts 2:31 and 1 Peter 3:19), a place where God had never gone before.

Just as experiencing evil for fallen created beings is helpful for them to permanently renew their relationship with the Creator-God (by influencing them to make a commitment to God that they will never break), so is God's experiencing temptation helpful for Him to understand the vulnerable condition of human beings for Himself (i.e., by having experienced it for Himself through Christ Jesus). Indeed, God's grace, forgiveness, and mercy flow through the shed blood of

Jesus Christ in God's understanding of just how weak human beings really are.

"Who Am I?"

The following two paragraphs are excerpted and edited from the present author's book entitled *Divine Metaphysics of Human Anatomy* (DMHA):

Regardless of the descriptors we might use personally to define ourselves, human beings individually think of themselves on the basis of what is "me" and "not me" (i.e., *self* and *nonself*) as well as what is "like me" and "not like me" (i.e., *like myself* and *not like myself*). It is from such thinking that human beings develop characteristics not only associated with individual identities but also associated with individual group identities. And it is from such thinking that human beings develop feelings about other human beings relative to whether they are: (1) similar and, therefore, familiar and perceived to be friendly; or (2) dissimilar and, therefore, unfamiliar and perceived to be unfriendly. Both hospitality and hostility toward others are dependent on such conclusions. [DMHA, page 31]

Metaphysically speaking, the family of God recognizes the difference between "Self" and "non-Self." Members of the family of God recognize who belongs to God and who does not. John the Baptist[10] alluded to the metaphysical difference between "Self" and "non-Self" when comparing Christ Jesus and himself; he declared: "He must increase, but I must decrease."[11] Members of the family of God must not only decrease in selfishness, willfulness, and vanity, they must exclude everything foreign to the identity of God from their individual, collective, and corporate consciousness. Although the number of

---

[10] *Iochanan the Baptizer* or *Yochanan the Immerser*

[11] John 3:30, King James Version

members within the family of God may vary, their basic characteristics and true nature remain the same. It is in this way that the family of God increases by decreasing, includes by excluding, and often varies yet never changes. As a child, the present author remembers hearing the great evangelist Kathryn Kuhlman make this prayer request to God during healing services: "Let there be less of me and more of Thee until there is none of me and all of Thee." In other words, let our false identity be lost and our true identity be found in Christ Jesus because He alone constitutes our Self. (This is not meant to imply that we are God or that we will ever become God.) [DMHA, page 218]

The two most important questions that have plagued members of the human race include: (1) "Who am I?" (i.e., "What is my true identity?"); and (2) "Why am I here?" (i.e., "What is my purpose for *being?*" or "Why do I exist?") Although there are components to the answers that may take time to settle within our consciousness, these questions are answered both immediately and simultaneously when we come to know who we are meant to be through the shed blood of the Lord Jesus Christ, the only-begotten Son of God. We then know that our sole identity is established in Jesus Christ and that our one true and only real identity in God is born of Jesus Christ. As soon as we fully understand who we are in God as His re-born and re-created beings through Jesus Christ, our only desires are: (1) to please God in obedience and self-discipline; (2) to worship God and do His Will; and (3) to bless God's Holy Name in our every thought, feeling, word, and deed. For every authentic Christian, there comes a day to not only proclaim but also believe: "It is no longer I who live but Christ who lives in me!" (Galatians 2:20a KJV Paraphrase) Such a belief comes in the recognition that God is our universal Self (regardless if this specific phraseology is used or not).

People who steadfastly choose to honor and glorify an abased, lower, or animal self have accepted a false self as their identity. Unfortunately, this false self eventually takes over and becomes their true self (i.e., who they really are). Such people demonstrate vulgarity, vanity, and violence in their lives and, therefore, are destined for eternal damnation. These are the ones who perish in their own corruption. (This is not to say that we should not try to reach them or try to help them recognize and experience an alternate approach to life.)

People who have chosen to honor and glorify a conscious functioning, composite, or human self have also accepted a false sense of self even though it may be a cultured, well-educated, generous, and courteous self. These people are destined to repeat their earthbound experiences until they finally get it completely wrong or completely right (i.e., by rejecting or accepting Jesus Christ as their personal Savior).

The only people who are completely right about who they are choose to manifest their higher self, supraself, or absolute identity in God. This requires denying both a lower self and a human self as an absolute identity. It requires souls in dust to reject both a carnal nature and a human nature and accept a divine nature as their only absolute reality. (This is not to say that we should pretend to be divine, or made of the substance of God, but that we should emulate only those characteristics that are pleasing to God.)

In the final analysis, we are who we think we are and who we act like we are.

Forgiving Ourselves

The present author understands what psychological counselors are trying to convey when they say that people must forgive themselves for their past mistakes. However, forgiving oneself is unnecessary if one accepts that the Lord's forgiveness is absolute when one has confessed to Him — and repented of — errant thoughts, feelings, words, and actions. In other words, one should no longer have guilt and emotional pain when one completely trusts in an omnipotent God's forgiveness. If God, our universal Self, has forgiven us and we accept His forgiveness, then there is no need to forgive oneself. When God has forgiven us, then "You" have forgiven you. ("You" here represents your true identity in God, who is your Self through the shed blood of Jesus Christ.) Who are we to tell God that He has not forgiven us when He has? Who are we to tell God that His decision is not absolute?

Feeling the need to forgive yourself indicates that your trust in God to forgive you is less than complete and perfect. Such feeling also indicates competition with God. If God is Sovereign (and *He is*), then we must accept His absolute power to absolve us of our confessed sins, debts, and trespasses. Other than our own repentance and confession to God, we do not need to insert ourselves additionally into the process of forgiveness. What God thinks and says always takes precedence over what we think and say. God's Will is supreme and sovereign.

Spiritual Provisions during Faith Development

The majority of people fail to understand the import of the expression "Son of God" when it is used for Jesus Christ. They don't quite get how its meaning differs from the meaning of the expression "Sons of God" when that expression is used for saved people in human flesh. Jesus Christ is the *only-begotten Son of God* because he is the only person ever conceived who did not have a biological father. To be sure, all people saved by accepting the Lord Jesus Christ as personal Savior are *Sons of God,* but they all had biological fathers.

In the ancient language of the Holy Bible, even women are considered "Sons of God" — not because of genitals and gender but because, in its ancient use, "Sons of God" really means "Heirs of God" or "Joint Heirs with Jesus Christ." At one time in the civil practices of patriarchal societies, males were the sole heirs of their fathers' possessions. Thus, based on the etymology of the expression "Sons of God," Christian women should not take umbrage at its use for them. Although well-intentioned people today sometimes try to fix past inequities by using gender-neutral language, sometimes the gender-neutral language does not carry the full significance of the originally-intended meaning. To be sure, "sons and daughters of God" is accurate but that expression loses the historical perspective of entitled inheritance. (Even though Job's daughters were included as his heirs, such an inclusion was quite unusual for that time — except, of course, when there were no male heirs.)

Jesus Christ is the "Son of God" because he is the only human being that was ever conceived by God's Holy Spirit in consort with a human female. Hence, Jesus Christ as the Son of God is the *only-begotten* Son of God. (In the ancient language of the Holy Bible, fathers "begat" children by contributing their *seed,* or sperm, to the process.) No human being was the father of Jesus Christ because God's Holy Spirit contributed the *seed.* Although people who are unable to conceptually understand supernatural events might look for natural explanations for the birth of Jesus Christ — *for example,* that his mother was a chimera[12] or that one of her two X-chromosomes had an inherited translocated Sex-determining region from a paternal Y-Chromosome (i.e., SRY gene).

Of course, the Author of all life could have supplied a complementary set of twenty-three chromosomes containing a Y chromosome at the time of Christ Jesus' conception. But no natural explanation is necessary to explain the conception of Jesus Christ to authentic Christians. Authentic Christians accept by faith the explanation of the virgin birth of Jesus Christ. Even with a set of 23 chromosomes supplied by God, the virgin birth can only be understood by faith — which is a spiritual and supernatural understanding. The understanding is also *meta*physical because it is *beyond* physical understanding.

Christians understand themselves to be *born again*, or spiritually reborn, based on their faith conversion in accepting that Jesus Christ is the only-begotten Son of God and the only Savior of the world —

---

[12] In the sense used here, a *chimera* is a human being that has been formed from two or more separate zygotes (fertilized eggs) that have fused together shortly after their fertilization.

whose death upon the cross is the only substitutionary sacrifice acceptable to God the Father for the forgiveness of their sins. Christians understand that their own spiritual conversion is only possible by God's Holy Spirit metaphysically depositing the seed of faith within them individually. Christians understand that such deposition was necessary in order for them to receive the knowledge of salvation. It is in the context of the deposition of the seed of faith within their souls that all Christians are the Sons of God. Even though every newborn human infant has redemptive value, a human being does not technically become a Son of God until he or she willingly accepts the Lord Jesus Christ as his or her personal Savior. Yes, faith is a gift from God, but, like the mother of Jesus Christ, we must each accept, and not reject, the metaphysical deposition of the seed of faith within us by God's Holy Spirit in order for our true spiritual life to begin.

Just as the developing human egg has covering layers of cells to help protect it, nourish it, and stabilize it, so is each *prospective* Christian protected, nourished, and stabilized until the time that he or she can make a decision for himself or herself to accept or reject Jesus Christ as personal Savior. (Acceptance of Jesus Christ as only-begotten Son of God and Savior occurs at the exact moment of one's spiritual fertilization by God's Holy Spirit; it is this event that begins our personal faith.) And just as the developing human embryo has extraembryonic membranes to protect it, nourish it, and stabilize it, so does the newly-born Christian *faith embryo* have spiritual protection, nourishment, and stability from the Creator-God throughout its entire spiritual development and maturation (i.e., its sanctification). Finally, just as the appearance of blood in the developing human embryo supports the conclusion that the embryo is alive physically, so does the metaphysical appearance of the shed blood of Jesus Christ within the consciousness of a saved person's developing *faith embryo* prove that the individual is alive spiritually.

Because the Holy Bible is clear that "life is in the blood" (Leviticus 17:11 KJV), the present author has concluded that the newly-conceived human embryo is not truly a living human being until the first instant that it produces histologically-identifiable blood cells, which occurs in the developing yolk sac sometime during the third week of development after the union of the egg (i.e., secondary oocyte) and fertilizing spermatozoon. To be sure, the cells of the human embryo during its first two weeks of ontogeny are living, but they do not constitute a living human being from the standpoint of Torah — if we use the presence of blood as the measure of life. Because the Holy Bible establishes that the Lord God Almighty is against the spilling of *innocent blood* (Deuteronomy 19:10), then, from a religious legalistic standpoint, abortion can only safely take place within the first two weeks after conception. The word *safely* here means "without spiritual consequences, or without invoking the wrath of God." Of course, all of this is moot if effective contraception has been used or if the person who has spilled innocent blood has done so in ignorance of this criterion and/or has asked for God's forgiveness.

Exercises and Activities in Christian Metaphysics

1. Where does the Creator-God reside?

2. How can we meet God and what preparation is involved?

3. Explain what *vulgar* means to you.

4. On a separate sheet of paper, discuss your own struggles with abuse-oriented, addiction-driven, and sexually-indulgent thoughts, feelings, ideas, images, and behaviors. As soon as you are satisfied with the accuracy of your answer, discuss it with your Creator and then burn it. (It is no one else's business.) If you are answering questions from this book to satisfy requirements for a course, then scotch tape a piece of the burnt fragment to your answer page to

show that you have answered this question (or take a digital photo of the burnt fragment and embed the picture in your digital document).

5. When do we enter into temptation?

6. Research "Word-of-faith" religious movements and list at least three spiritually-helpful tenets and three spiritually-harmful tenets that are associated with them.

7. How do we quell desires to do that which is dishonoring to ourselves and others as well as dishonoring to God?

8. How does the mortal mind in Satan interact with the carnal mind in human beings to lead them to sin against God by transgressing His Will?

9. What will cause human beings to sin during the Millennium of Peace while Satan's evil forces are incarcerated in the bottomless Pit?

10. How does God's Holy Spirit relate to the power to resist temptation?

11. Why is it helpful to include the word *Satan's* with the noun phrase "mortal mind"? And why is it helpful to include the word *God's* with the noun phrase "divine Mind"?

12. This textbook uses Judas Iscariot as an example of someone for whom Satan became his *self.* Name another person from history for whom Satan became his or her *self.* Explain your choice. And

explain how you can be certain that the person you chose was beyond reclamation (i.e., eternally damned).

13. Conduct a self-assessment using the five states of mind that give Satan's mortal mind an opportunity to broadcast unwholesome and unclean messages to us. Share the self-assessment with a trustworthy spiritual elder and have the elder initial a blank line for your answer to question 13. (Do not share your self-assessment with your instructor even if you consider him or her to be a trustworthy spiritual elder.)

14. Write a short essay of approximately two hundred words on the subject of Christian metaphysics as it relates to trust in God.

15. What is the difference between *jealousy* and *envy?*

16. Review the Ten Commandments and decide if jealousy, envy, both, or neither is the basis for each commandment. Construct a table that summarizes your conclusions.

17. Explain the roles of unforgiveness and forgiveness in one's spiritual life.

18. In what way or ways does bitterness act as an impediment to spiritual growth and development?

19. What are we to leave behind in preparation for going to Heaven?

20. Give at least two additional examples of entering into temptation other than the four examples already given in Chapter Two.

21. What keeps us from fulfilling our destiny in God? Please explain.

22. Why must we be on guard especially during sleep, sleep deprivation, and general fatigue?

23. Give at least two examples of using Christian metaphysics in a practical way.

24. Take the three questions that God might ask you after you have willingly entered a state of temptation and rephrase them so that you are asking yourself.

25. Just as experiencing evil for fallen created beings is helpful for them to permanently reject evil and renew their relationship with the Creator-God, so is God's experiencing temptation helpful for Him to personally understand the extremely vulnerable condition of human beings. Because the two concepts relating to experiential levels of understanding are somewhat unusual, discuss them to demonstrate your practical understanding of them.

26. From the standpoint of Christian metaphysics, what is the difference between *Self* and *non-Self?*

27. Using Christian metaphysics, provide answers to these two questions: "Who am I?" and "Why am I here on Earth?"

28. Should we "write off" all people who are vulgar, vain, and violent?

29. Why don't we need to forgive ourselves of our trespasses, sins, and debts?

30. Considering the etymology of *Sons of God,* are Christian women metaphysically *Sons of God?* Please explain.

31. What enabled you to become *born-again?*

32. What proves that a *faith embryo* is alive?

33. From a Biblical standpoint, when is the developing physical embryo considered a living being? (Of course, you may disagree with the present author's perspective.)

Chapter Three

States of Mind

Definitions

In one of the present author's earlier books, entitled *Divine Metaphysics of Human Anatomy*, he defined *mind* as "creative consciousness."[13] For the purposes of this book, the word *mind* is defined more explicitly as "consciousness with volition (i.e., awareness with free will or the power to choose) and the ability to execute that volition in one's imagination and through one's actions." In its broadest sense, the word *mind* may be used synonymously with the phrase *creative consciousness,* but the essence of the word *mind* and its extended meanings and nuances are more complex. (A more expanded, metaphysical definition of *consciousness* will be given in Chapter Seven of this book.)

As in the present author's previous written work, the word *mind* here is also used interchangeably with the word *spirit* — not only, *for example,* in *Mind* and *Spirit* (i.e., the Mind of God and God's Holy Spirit) but also that which is, *generally speaking,* invisible as well as independent of biological processes associated with neuroanatomy, neurophysiology, and neuroendocrinology. "Generally speaking" is used here because *carnal mind* is greatly dependent on fleshly existence as well as on human frailties, weaknesses, and vulnerabilities. "Generally speaking" is also used here because, in this book, the noun phrase *human mind* is used interchangeably with the

---

[13] *Divine Metaphysics of Human Anatomy* by Rev. Joseph Adam Pearson, Ph.D., Christ Evangelical Bible Institute, Copyright 2018, ISBN 978-0985772819, page 98.

noun phrase *human brain*. Although human beings are more than physical beings, and the consciousness that human beings have access to is well beyond that delineated by the human brain, the word *human* used as a qualifier for *mind* is constraining in itself by referring to only one level of consciousness (i.e., the earth plane, or human level, of consciousness). To be sure, a superior human intellect may be valuable spiritually but only when it is channeling and processing the thoughts, feelings, ideas, and images of one's higher self, supraself, or absolute identity in God.

In this book, there are five general states of mind: (1) God's divine Mind, (2) the mind of one's electromagnetic, or spirit, body,[14] (3) the human mind, (4) the carnal mind, and (5) the mortal mind of Satan, his fallen angels, and his unclean spirits.

1. God's divine Mind (also known as the *Mind of God* and the *Mind of Christ*) governs the entire universe spiritually and physically. It is the creative consciousness of God — which is to say, the Supraconsciousness of the Creator. The free will, or volition, of God's divine Mind is supreme and sovereign to the individual and collective wills of all other beings, unfallen or fallen.

2. The mind of one's electromagnetic, or spirit, body is the central energy core that serves as the seat of consciousness for the soul; this invisible mind provides an interface between one's human mind and God's divine Mind as well as between one's human mind and Satan's mortal mind. Although this control center provides interfaces for the human mind, its functionality in no way depends on the human brain for its existence. Discarnates (souls without a human body) are able to think, feel, imagine, and make decisions using this mind. This mind determines the personality, attitude, and affect (emotions or mood) of one's soul.

---

[14] The *electromagnetic body* can also be referred to as the *inner body*, the *invisible body*, or the *spirit body*.

3. The human mind with its potential for intellectual analysis and its capability for emotional connectivity is dependent on the human brain, its neuroanatomy, neurophysiology, and neuroendocrinology. The human mind is superior to the minds, brains, and neural networks of all other animals. Because the human mind/human brain is superior, it provides a suitable habitation for the human soul.

4. The carnal mind is the vapid consciousness of a mortal being's animal, lower, or abased self. Although "mortal being" might imply "corporeal being" (or an *incarnate*) to most readers, in the sense that the noun phrase is used in this textbook, "mortal being" refers to any fallen created being regardless of its incarnate or discarnate state. Left to its own devices in an incarnate mortal being, the carnal mind is responsible for that mortal being's complete depravity and instinct gone wild.

5. The mortal mind of Satan, his fallen angels, and his unclean spirits is the fragmented awareness that comes from spiritual death, or permanent separation from the Creator-God (i.e., the second death). This mind is absolutely cunning as well as unreservedly self-serving and evil; it fans the flames of unclean desires associated with the carnal mind. This mind transforms complete depravity to absolute, focused evil. The mind that is absolutely evil derives pleasure from attacking others, hurting others, and murdering others emotionally, mentally, physically, and spiritually.

To be sure, there can be overlap between the five states of mind just described and the consciousness, or awareness, they each possess. *For example,* carnal mind and Satan's mortal mind have a symbiotic relationship with each other. Because they are both outside of the Will of God, Satan's mortal mind is able to easily read the carnal mind of a person's lower, abased, or animal self. Then, Satan's mortal mind is able to target the person's specific weaknesses and vulnerabilities by constructing images and scenarios that play to them (i.e., the weaknesses and vulnerabilities) in the person's imagination. Satan's mortal mind uses our imaginations to try to engage us and get us to respond favorably to the temptations it constructs. If we end up grabbing the bait, we are pulled — hook, line, and sinker — into a state of addictive sin. As we mature spiritually in Christ Jesus, we eventually choose to no longer entertain and indulge the unclean desires of the carnal mind in our lower, abased, or animal self. When we learn to say "No!" to our unclean desires, we end up not only changing our present and future but also changing our past. When we finally say "No!" to a temptation that has plagued us, this reaction reaches back through relative time, actually altering space-time by removing a particular unclean desire from the person's soul.

Each unclean desire that we manifest is representative of a warp in our soul. Although we are forgiven by accepting the shed blood of Jesus Christ as atonement for our sins, each saved soul still retains warps in it either until it transitions to a heavenly plane of consciousness through physical death or until it learns to overcome its individual warps, or unclean desires, through the power of that shed blood while it is still on Earth.

Without the qualifier of "God's" in *God's divine Mind* and of "Satan's" in *Satan's mortal mind,* the reader or hearer might misconclude that these two general states of mind are only impersonal supernatural forces. However, neither is the one true and only real God impersonal nor is Satan, the Enemy of God, impersonal. Both God's mind and Satan's mind are personal because they are associated with beings that have free will, or volition. Both the Creator-God and His eternal enemy, Satan, each have the ability to act on the free will that functions as a part of their individual consciousness. Of course, the consciousness of God constitutes the deepest, highest, and noblest levels of consciousness possible and the consciousness of Satan constitutes the most superficial, lowest, and vilest levels of consciousness possible. The consciousness of God is spiritually enlightened and metaphysically explosive in its creativity, and the consciousness of Satan is spiritually enblackened and metaphysically implosive in its self-absorption. The first is resident in spiritual Light and the second is resident in spiritual Darkness. Metaphysically speaking, God's divine Mind is a continuously-expanding supernova and Satan's mortal mind is a continually-inverting black hole. Depending on which one has control over one's personal being, God's spiritual Light can expunge Satan's spiritual Darkness and Satan's spiritual Darkness can eclipse God's spiritual Light. Whereas the interaction of God's divine Mind and the human mind demonstrates supernatural mutualism, the interaction of Satan's mortal mind and the human mind can only demonstrate supernatural parasitism because, in such a relationship, the human spirit is always denigrated, hurt, and harmed at the same time that Satan's mortal mind is fed and nourished.

Earlier in this book, in the subsection entitled "When Satan becomes our *self,*" the present author first wrote that carnal mind "is the intellect of the lower, abased, or animal self." To be sure, there is considerable overlap between the brain and carnal mind in human beings because carnal mind involves portions of the brain's limbic system and brain stem coupled with those areas of the brain's prefrontal cerebral cortex that govern volition. However, carnal mind has spiritual aspects to it, too. Carnal mind and its associated desires can exist in the world of the invisible. *For example,* (1) the Holy Bible is clear that some angels of God fell from heaven because they materialized in human form specifically to have sexual intercourse with mortal beings. Carnal mind was in operation in them even though they were not in corporeality at the time these desires took shape. To be sure, because of this transgression, these fallen angels have been incarcerated by God in "the bottomless Pit," awaiting their final damnation to the Lake of Fire at the time of the Great White Throne Judgment of God.[15] And (2) carnal mind is also present in reprobate discarnate souls (i.e., unclean spirits, demons, and devils) who no longer have a human brain although they each possessed a human brain while they were incarnate (i.e., before they became discarnate demons). In fact, it is because they were once incarnate that reprobate discarnate souls retain a carnal mind and its associated desires; as a result, they seek to act on their carnal desires in the only

---

[15] Study the following passages from the Holy Bible: Genesis 6:1-6:4; Jude 1:6; Revelation 20:11 & 14.

ways they can — by influencing, controlling, and possessing human beings for this purpose.

Almost everyone underestimates the role of unclean spirits in influencing human beings to act on carnal desires. Metaphysically speaking, unclean spirits are like salamanders and chameleons because they are able to stick to — and blend in with — background scenery on the platform of the human mind; to be sure, unclean spirits possess elusive abilities. Unclean spirits are even able to portray themselves as benevolent, tender, and helpful characters in our imaginations in order to get us to entertain and indulge the unclean desires of our carnal mind. Unclean spirits cunningly build scenarios into our night dreams and daydreams that may seem only slightly off-color or even defensible given our current life situations. They do this in an effort to cause us to conclude that wrong things are right in order to gain our moral approval. They want to move us to first do the wrong thing in our imaginations (e.g., fornication, adultery, theft, substance abuse, boasting, etc.) so that we will then more easily act it out reflexively in our flesh. Unclean spirits will flatter us, portray themselves as something they are not, or bully us by waging false accusations at us. In short, unclean spirits will do whatever is necessary to get us to do what they want. To fight unclean spirits most successfully, we must be willing to raise a banner for our Creator-God and never let it down. Raising such a banner requires hypervigilance.

Unclean spirits are spiritually ubiquitous. Spiritually-ungrounded human beings who are uniquely sensitive to realms of the invisible are not the only prey for unclean spirits. All unclean spirits are predatory and seek to capture the thinking, feeling, and mental imaging of every human being. Unclean spirits interact with carnal mind at the level of our human desires to do the wrong thing (i.e., act in undisciplined and disobedient ways). As long as we desire to satisfy impure motives, unholy attitudes, and addictive behaviors, we attract unclean spirits to us and provide a suitable mental habitation for them. Depending on the depth and scope of our unclean desires, we unwittingly invite unclean spirits to participate in our unclean thoughts, emotions, ideations, imagery, and actions. As unclean spirits interact with our own carnal desires, they try to withhold from us what is rightfully ours in the Lord God Almighty.

Yes, unclean spirits have considerable influence on the human psyche (i.e., mind or spirit), but we must first override and overcome our own unclean desires in order to be rid of influences from unclean spirits. We can only override and overcome unclean desires by: (1) praying without ceasing; (2) constantly checking our desires to make sure that we are focused on obeying God's Will and pleasing Him; (3) choosing to no longer entertain and indulge unclean desires; and (4) deciding to serve the Lord Jesus Christ regardless of personal cost — not only during the remainder of our human life but throughout all eternity. Regularly entertaining and indulging the desires of our carnal mind sets the stage for Satan's mortal mind to be in control of us, especially through the unclean spirits that belong to him.

When tempted by unclean desires in daydreams and night dreams, repeat the following statement (but only if the statement is true for you): "By the power in the shed blood of my Lord and Savior, Jesus Christ, and in the power of the Name of my Lord and Savior, Jesus Christ, I choose to no longer entertain and indulge unclean desires because I am committed to follow my Lord and Savior, Jesus Christ, not only throughout the rest of my earthly days but throughout all eternity as well."

Our own unclean desires become so natural to us that we sometimes subconsciously, or unconsciously, welcome them back as old friends. In this way, we unwittingly welcome unclean spirits into the dark, spiritually-malignant spots in our consciousness. Although demons may present themselves as familiar and friendly spirits, they are our eternal enemies. (Once they capture our attention, their pretended good nature and humor soon turn to biting mockery and derision.)

The human mind may be used as an instrument of God's divine Mind or as an instrument of Satan's mortal mind — although not synchronously or simultaneously. Based on the conscious choice of one's personal being, either God's divine Mind or Satan's mortal mind (even in our default or passive submission to it) has control. One or the other has control but not both at the same time. This does not mean that, if God's divine Mind has control, one cannot become aware of the thoughts, feelings, ideas, and images of Satan's mortal mind. Conversely, this does not mean that, if Satan's mortal mind has control, one cannot become aware of the thoughts, feelings, ideas, and images of God's divine Mind. The thoughts, feelings, ideas, and images of Satan's mortal mind can break, or burst forth, into the human mind to interrupt our communion with the Supraconsciousness of God; and the thoughts, feelings, ideas, and images of God's divine Mind can break, or burst forth, into the human mind — even after we have willingly entered into the substate, or substratum, of Satan's mortal mind where temptation occurs.

God, God's holy angels, and God's heavenly saints communicate electromagnetically with the human being — which is to say, God's divine Mind communicates directly with the central core of our electromagnetic body (i.e., our invisible, inner, or spirit body). Likewise, Satan, his fallen angels, and his unclean spirits communicate electromagnetically with the human being — which is to say, Satan's mortal mind also communicates directly with the central core of our electromagnetic body. (Every human being has an electromagnetic body.) Communication from God's divine Mind or Satan's mortal mind with one's electromagnetic body is then translated into words and images in one's human brain. The human brain processes the translated words and images and acts on them in one's imagination and, often (but not always), through one's corporeality. Through this process of translation, we integrate (i.e., accommodate and assimilate) either the thoughts of God or the thoughts of Satan into our own personal consciousness. Thus, we end up ultimately identifying with one or the other. Eventually, we end up identifying completely with God's divine Mind or Satan's mortal mind.

In the final analysis, we are who we see ourselves to be. To be sure, we choose our final identity and the ultimate reality in which we live. Unless we consciously choose God's divine Mind, we will not fulfill the destiny that the Creator-God has planned for us nor will we fit into the place He has prepared for us throughout all eternity.

Satan's Mortal Mind

In written works by other authors, the noun phrase *carnal mind* is sometimes used interchangeably with the noun phrase *mortal mind*. To be sure, when *carnal mind* and *mortal mind* are each described as "consciousness that is not governed by the Spirit of God," the two phrases are identical in meaning. However, the present author makes a distinction between the two phrases based on the different nuances of meaning for *carnal* and *mortal*. Because the word *carnal* means "flesh, or fleshly," the manifestations of *carnal mind* are entirely dependent on material existence (even though the causality and operations of *carnal mind* are dependent on both material and spiritual existence). In contrast, because the word *mortal* means "dead, or deadly," the manifestations of *mortal mind* are not dependent on material existence because they may take place in the physical realm, the spiritual realm, or both (even though the causality and operations of *mortal mind* occur solely in the spiritual realm). From the standpoint of Christian metaphysics posited in this book, although there can be overlap in the meanings of *carnal mind* and *mortal mind,* the two phrases are *not* perfectly synonymous.

As mentioned earlier, because of its relationship to the limbic system, brain stem, and prefrontal cerebral cortex, *carnal mind* is an extension of the human mind, or human brain. C*arnal mind* depends on the physical senses and what we individually pursue as a result of personally processing the input from those senses. To be sure, one can think of *carnal mind* as the depraved human mind that establishes intellect for the lower, animal, or abased self, but one can also think of *carnal* mind as the mind that establishes instinct for most vertebrates (i.e., *for example,* in the so-called *reptilian* and *rat brain portions of the human brain).* In contrast to *carnal mind,* which manifests physically as evil (acknowledging here that unclean desires always precede evil actions in corporeality), *mortal mind* manifests spiritually as evil.

To be sure, evil is evil; however, the ways that carnal mind and mortal mind each manifest evil are different although, at times, there can be considerable overlap of the two: *For example,* when a human being exercises its carnal mind, it is an open invitation for Satan's mortal mind to collaborate in its depravity; and as demonic discarnate beings exercise Satan's mortal mind, they intend their thoughts, feelings, ideas, and images to impinge on the depraved human mind and influence the human being to act beyond the scope of its own depraved personal desires. That Judas Iscariot gave free reign to his carnal mind not only permitted and allowed Satan to work through him, it invited Satan's mortal mind to enter into him. This also describes the interaction of carnal mind and mortal mind in every tyrannical despot and in every serial killer that has ever lived. To be sure, people influenced by Satan's mortal mind to perform evil deeds are not relieved of their own responsibility for permitting, allowing, and inviting such things to happen.

In summary, although *carnal mind* is dependent on corporeality for its manifestations, *mortal mind* is independent of corporeality for its manifestations. Regardless, Satan's mortal mind is eager to accommodate the unclean desires of the human carnal mind; and the human carnal mind is eager to accommodate the unclean desires of Satan's mortal mind. It is only God's divine Mind through the indwelling presence of His Holy Spirit that keeps us from acting on any unclean desire.

God's Divine Mind

God's divine Mind possesses the deepest, highest, and noblest levels of spiritually-enlightened consciousness possible. For this reason, God's creative consciousness may be described as the Supraconsciousness of the Creator, or Supraconsciousness-in-itself.

The Supraconsciousness of the Creator is the *Summum Bonum* of awareness and, thus, omnipresent and omniscient. The verbiage of *omnipresent* and *omniscient* has practical significance to the Christian believer because it reinforces the absolute truth that God's creative consciousness is sovereign and supreme. Because God's divine Mind is able to act without any hindrance or limitation, it is also *omnipotent.* As God acts in His imagination (i.e., *wills* something to happen), God's imagined action is translated instantaneously into reality, including corporeal reality if that is what the Creator-God desires. Any word expressed in God's divine Mind takes shape, and is fulfilled spiritually and/or physically, without a lag in time.

God's divine Mind makes God's Will known and understandable to created beings by striking chords of truth that resonate within the electromagnetic fibers and energy vortices of their very being. God's divine Mind makes God's thoughts, feelings, ideas, and images known to created beings either directly through God's Spirit or indirectly through God's heavenly messengers. God the Father purposely keeps His distance from corporeal beings so that His Fiery Presence does not expunge or annihilate them. Indeed, God partitioned Himself into Father, Son, and Holy Spirit so that He could communicate with salvageable fallen created beings without destroying them. (God also uses heavenly messengers for the same reason.)

God's divine Mind communicates with human beings by interacting with their electromagnetic bodies. (The souls and spirits of created beings are contained within these invisible spirit bodies.) The interactions of the thoughts, feelings, ideas, and images from God's divine Mind with the electromagnetic body of a human being are then translated into what is perceived and apprehended by the human brain in symbology — including the imagery, semantics, and syntax associated with language. Sometimes, human beings willingly ignore the import of what is communicated to them. And sometimes they misread the symbology of the communicated thoughts, feelings, ideas, and images from God's divine Mind because they have not properly pondered its meaning long enough or are not yet mature enough to understand it metaphysically.

Human beings experience supernatural ecstasy and spiritual euphoria when they permit their conscious functioning self to step aside and allow their higher self, or supraself, to take over. Supernatural ecstasy and spiritual euphoria translate as happiness and joy within the human mind and spirit. Fasting, penitence, and prayer often induce a trance-like state during which intense feelings of well-being are engendered. When we delight in our Creator-God, He delights in us. When we rejoice in Him, He rejoices in us. Out-of-body experiences (i.e., *astral projection*), prophetic dreams, supernatural visions, and spiritual glimpses of the truth occur when the supraself is in control.

The reason that there can be power in pain and suffering is because pain and suffering force us to look beyond our human selves in order for us to retain and maintain our mental equilibrium and emotional composure. During such times of *looking beyond,* we become more aware of the thoughts, feelings, ideas, and images of God's divine Mind. This does not mean that we should seek pain and suffering; it means that we should radically rely on God especially when we experience pain and suffering. As a result, there will be a breakthrough for us relative to spiritual apprehension and comprehension.

There is a spiritual law that has been established in God's divine Mind that has to do with rejection and denigration by others. God has decreed that all who are rejected and denigrated for His sake will end up becoming an integral part of the cornerstone, or centerpiece, of His divine Plan. That Christ Jesus became the *chief* cornerstone, or primary centerpiece, of God's spiritual universe not only attests to the existence of this spiritual law but also to its fulfillment. Therefore, if you have been undervalued, you should rejoice; undervaluing often precipitates success in God. In fact, rejection, denigration, and undervaluing always guarantee spiritual success when their challenge is met in the Lord and when enduring them honors the Lord:

{11} Blessed are you, when people revile you, and persecute you, and say all manner of evil against you falsely, for my sake. {12} Rejoice and be exceedingly glad: for great is your reward in heaven: for so persecuted were the prophets before you.

Matthew 5:11-12 KJV Paraphrase

In contrast, when we believe the lies from Satan's mortal mind about our lack of worth and value, we open ourselves up to further demonic attack, manipulation, and exploitation. Consequently, we need to remind ourselves regularly that we always have Self-worth and Self-value in God's divine Mind.

God chose David to slay Goliath because David was undervalued by others. Selecting David helped God prove to fallen created beings that He is capable of doing anything through anyone. And it was being undervalued by others that helped shape David's heart for the Lord. God takes what is seemingly insignificant and makes it significant. God takes what is ridiculed and places it in a position of honor. God does this so that no human being can boast of his or her own abilities. Indeed, God's strength is made perfect in our weaknesses, infirmities, and rejections.

If we individually seek to make a name for ourselves on Earth, Satan's mortal mind *can* overtake and use us. However, if we seek to promote the Name of our Lord and Savior, Jesus Christ, *instead of our own names,* then God *will* use us.

The Power of Chronic Physical Pain

In general, adversity is a wonderful stimulus for spiritual growth. More specifically, chronic physical pain has power in it for those who meet its challenge daily in the Lord because such pain requires us to look beyond it — that is, heavenward — in order to overcome it. To be sure, God's strength is made perfect in our weakness. Although people who do not have chronic physical pain might think that they know what it is, they can never know what it is until they experience it for themselves. Unless they experience it for themselves, they will either trivialize it or think that it does not really exist at the level that it does.

There is a big spiritual payout for those who have chronic physical pain and meet its challenges daily in the Lord. *For example:* (1) experiencing chronic physical pain helps us to see beyond our individual corporeal, or human, identities; (2) experiencing chronic physical pain clears the platform of our mind from sinful desires; and (3) experiencing chronic physical pain helps us to become more like God (remember that we were originally made in the image and likeness of God) by joining us to the crucified Christ. Additional explanations are given in the following three examples:

1. A personal testimony from the present author:

    On the evening of April 1, 2013, I finally admitted to myself that I had substantial, recurring pain in my left arm, shoulder, and back. (People who practice positive thinking in many of its various forms often do not like to admit to themselves that they have physical pain because they do not want to mentally project defeat.) Immediately, I realized that just because I had pain in my arm, shoulder, and back did not mean that I had pain in my higher self, supraself, or absolute identity in God. In other words, the pain helped me to not only see that I am *not* my arm, shoulder, and back but also that I am not my physical body in any of its parts or even in its entirety. The pain helped me to look beyond the physical to see metaphysically. Of course, I am in corporeality, but even if I were to become a quadriplegic, I would still *not* be limited by my human body because I am *not* my human body. My human body is not my Self. Rather, God is my Self. I have my one true and only real identity in the Creator-God and not in my human body! To be sure, if I were quadriplegic, I would want to be physically restored and healed, but if I were not restored and healed I would not hold it against God. How could I? God is my Self. (Remember, stating that God is my Self is not saying that I am or can be God.)

2. The power we have in experiencing chronic physical pain goes well beyond the endogenous opioids our brains make to help counteract physical pain naturally. Chronic physical pain moves us into a realm where we can better explore who we really are spiritually. Paradoxically, we can become less chained to corporeality through

what the pain stimulates in us supernaturally. In other words, experiencing chronic physical pain helps clear the stage of the human mind of all thoughts, feelings, ideas, and images unrelated to pain because the brain only has enough room for experiencing just one strong emotion at a time. Consequently, because there is no room for anything other than experiencing a high level of pain, we have to fight to replace the pain with any thought, feeling, idea, or image that is unrelated to it. Because we must use considerable energy to replace the pain with something not related to it, the condition of chronic physical pain requires us to become highly selective of that on which we choose to focus. Generally speaking, people with chronic physical pain do not choose to entertain sinful thoughts, feelings, ideas, or images; instead, they usually choose to focus on more practical issues, including performing the mundane tasks they once took for granted. In this way, chronic physical pain can help move us beyond our addictions to sinful desires because it prompts us to think metaphysically.

3. When people who experience chronic physical pain focus on pleasing God rather than themselves, God permits their higher self, supraself, or absolute identity in Him to step in and take over. People with chronic physical pain will then experience a supernatural ecstasy and spiritual euphoria that enable them to transcend the pain they have been experiencing. In this way, chronic physical pain helps us to become more like God (not become God but become more *like* God) by experiencing a more intimate relationship with Him. It is no accident that many who have experienced chronic physical pain, and who daily met its challenges in the Lord, fulfilled their destiny in God as true seers, mystics, oracles, visionaries, and prophets of God. Thus does chronic physical pain enable us to look beyond the physical to the metaphysical.

Exercises and Activities in Christian Metaphysics

1. Provide definitions for *mind* and *consciousness* that are complementary to Christian metaphysics.

2. Does *carnal mind* only operate in human flesh (i.e., corporeality)? Explain when and in whom *carnal mind* operates.

3. Construct a simple table with the names of the five general states of mind in a column to the left and, in a column to the right, indicate if each mind operates in the realm of the visible alone, the invisible alone, or both the visible and the invisible. Because the descriptors may vary based on each student's perspective, briefly justify the labels *(visible, invisible,* or *both visible and invisible)* that you have used for each of the five states of mind. (There is room for variations in the answer to this question.)

4. Considering all of the combinations of the five general states of mind, indicate in which of these pairs *(a* through *j)* there may be some overlap and explain why: (a) God's divine Mind and the mind of the electromagnetic, or spirit, body; (b) God's divine Mind and the human mind; (c) God's divine Mind and the carnal mind; (d) God's divine Mind and Satan's mortal mind; (e) the mind of the electromagnetic, or spirit, body and the human mind; (f) the mind of the electromagnetic, or spirit, body and the carnal mind; (g) the mind of the electromagnetic, or spirit, body and Satan's mortal mind; (h) the human mind and the carnal mind; (i) the human mind and Satan's mortal mind; and (j) the carnal mind and Satan's mortal mind. If any of the previous pairs have no overlap, then simply write "no overlap" for them.

5. Is God a Being, a force, or both? Please explain your answer.

6. Is Satan a being, a force, or both? Please explain your answer.

7. What constitutes a *being?*

8. How does the consciousness of God's divine Mind differ from the consciousness of Satan's mortal mind?

9. In what way or ways does carnal mind have spiritual aspects to it?

10. What role do unclean spirits play in our entertaining and indulging unclean desires? Please explain.

11. How can we override and overcome unclean desires?

12. How do we combat unclean spirits?

13. With whom do you personally identify? Please explain.

14. How do we fulfill the destiny that the Creator-God has planned for us?

15. When are definitions for the two phrases *carnal mind* and *mortal mind* identical?

16. Construct a simple Venn diagram showing what you think is the overlap in meaning of the two phrases *carnal mind* and *mortal mind.*

17. What is the difference between evil that manifests physically and evil that manifests spiritually?

18. In addition to Judas Iscariot, list at least five other historical figures who have had Satan's mortal mind unmistakably working in them. Please explain the reason(s) for each choice.

19. Is *carnal mind* dependent on or independent of corporeality? Please explain.

20. Is *mortal mind* dependent on or independent of corporeality? Please explain.

21. What is the practical significance that the creative consciousness of God is described as *Supraconsciousness?*

22. Why did God partition Himself into Father, Son, and Holy Spirit?

23. Explain the mechanisms or processes involved in God's communication with human beings.

24. What is required for our supraself to be in control?

25. In what way or ways are rejection and denigration by others helpful to us spiritually? In what way or ways can they be harmful to us?

26. Why does God choose to use seemingly insignificant people?

27. How can chronic pain be valuable to us metaphysically?

Chapter Four

Whom Shall We Seek to Please?

Control and Possession

Most people seek to please themselves, some people seek to please others, and a few people seek to please God. In this book, "to please" means "to satisfy by doing someone's will." If you seek to please yourself, then you seek to satisfy yourself by doing your own will. If you seek to please others, then you seek to satisfy others by doing their will. If you seek to please God, then you seek to satisfy God by doing His Will. Ironically, it is only by seeking to please God that we really end up pleasing ourselves and others.

Most people seek to satisfy themselves because they want to be in control of their own circumstances and in possession of their own destiny. Some people seek to satisfy others because they are afraid of them, they want to manipulate them, and/or they genuinely want to help them. The few who seek to satisfy God recognize that they were created solely for the purpose of pleasing God by doing God's Will. The psalmist confirms: "Know that Yahweh has made us and not we ourselves" (Psalm 100:3 KJV Paraphrase). Although the saved in Christ receive God's Holy Spirit at the moment of their personal salvation, and although God will infuse the saved in Christ with His Glory when God the Son presents a revivified and reunified creation to God the Father at the end of the Millennium of Peace, all created beings in the Kingdom of God remain created beings eternally. We eternally remain created beings and God eternally remains our Creator. Our future fusion with God is really an interfaced admixture of God's Being and our own corporate being in Christ. Throughout all eternity, our individual identities as created beings are seen by God collectively as one composite image and separately as multiple compound images — all at the same time.

Although there are some Christians who might label the view that "our future fusion with God is really an admixture of God's Being and our own corporate being in Christ" as representative of Christoplatonism, "Eastern" religions, Gnostic mysticism, or New Ageism, they would do so because they fail to look at possibilities beyond physical referents — that is, beyond relative space-time. It is not the position of the present author that matter is evil. It is the position of the present author that evil is evil and that evil is, first and foremost, spiritual and invisible. Matter is neither our natural enemy nor our supernatural enemy; evil is our enemy. Ironically, there are those who would try to discredit Christian metaphysical views by claiming that matter must be good because God said that His entire creation was "good" (Genesis 1:31 KJV). The word "ironically" is used here because God called everything good *before* the Fall — so we cannot be certain what God's original creation looked like nor what life looked like in the Garden of Eden (i.e., Paradise). The word "ironically" is also used here because many people who fancy that they use Christian metaphysics (regardless of the nomenclature they use to represent it) use the same Biblical passage to support their claims that, because God called everything good, evil cannot exist. In order to view life metaphysically, we need to be willing to consider that, although all created beings in the future "new heaven and new earth"[16] have substance, are tangible, and possess somatic identities, their substance, tangibility, and somatic nature do not rely on physicality, materiality, or corporeality as we know it.

In the metaphysical reality of God, there is no discrete "me" because our personal identities are lost as well as found in God. Remember,

---

[16] Although fallen created beings who are now saved (both those on Earth as well as those already in Heaven) will receive their new bodies when Christ Jesus returns to Earth, all remaining created beings who are destined for the Kingdom of God will have their new bodies at the time that there is "a new heaven and a new earth" (Revelation 21:1 KJV).

God is *our universal Self.* In the metaphysical reality of God, there is no discrete "you" because our collective and corporate identities constitute a composite "us all" in Him. In other words, the people of God are not really separate from one another. The prayer that Christ Jesus modeled for us declares: "*our* Father" as well as "give *us,*" "forgive *us,*" "lead *us,*" and "deliver *us.*" In the same prayer, we are taught that God gives us "*our* daily bread" and forgiveness for "*our* debts, or trespasses." Christ's prayer does not use singular pronouns but plural pronouns (i.e., *our, us,* and *we).* Remember, our Self in God is *universal.* Therefore, God is *our universal Self.* In the metaphysical reality of God, when we pray using Christ's model, we ask God on behalf of *us all.* Although we retain individual identities in Heaven in addition to our collective and corporate identities, we will no longer think of ourselves in terms of "me" and "you." In Heaven, we will only use "me" and "you" or "us" and "them" when we are referring to ourselves versus the enemies of God (i.e., Satan, his fallen angels, his unclean spirits, and human beings who intractably deny that Jesus Christ is the only-begotten Son of God and Lord of us all). "Us all" here does not represent a geopolitical social organism; "us all" represents our metaphysical reality in God.

There is one Lord and one Master, but those who do God's Will are lords and masters. There is only one true and only real power and we have access to it provided that we submit ourselves in humility and gratitude to that power. We may tell Satan's mortal mind, his fallen angels, and his unclean spirits to depart from us in the Name of Jesus Christ, but we are not to tell our Creator-God anything except how sorry we are for our transgressions and how much we love Him.

We can share our thoughts, feelings, likes, and dislikes with our Creator-God. And we can *ask* Him for almost anything. But we are never to *tell* God what He should do. That would be unseemly. The problem with some "Word-of-faith" and "prosperity" movements is that, in effect, they *tell* God what to do. When we tell God what He should do, we are lacking humility as well as understanding of what the bigger picture looks like to our Creator-God.

When we overcome our major character deficits, they become our major character strengths. Our strengths are to be shared with others who are spiritually weak, immature, and underdeveloped. We must not take their trials and tribulations away from them or solve their problems for them; we can only show them how to overcome for themselves and how to solve their own problems for themselves by relying radically on God. We should challenge others with the truth but only to the degree that others value the truth. The truth is a blinding light to those who do not want to see it because they do not value it. True introspection requires shining light on those areas within our minds that were previously in the dark and had *sin spots* on them.

We can only achieve our greatest goals by presenting our spiritual gifts to the Lord God Almighty for His pleasure. If our goals include our own personal celebrity, fame, convenience, leisure, and material wealth, then we are seeking to achieve our goals for our own pleasure and purpose and not for God's. We must check our motives at our portal of thought to evaluate them and discard them if they are selfish and willful. Because our own carnal desires and the evil desires of unclean spirits and Satan's mortal mind are ever-ready to rob us of our goals for God, we must learn our vulnerabilities so that we can continually present them to the Lord God Almighty for His mercy and strength in order to overcome them. We overcome them: (1) by living in a state of perpetual contrition, (2) by resisting unclean desires, and (3) by quickly replacing unclean desires with our overriding desire to please the Lord God Almighty. When you are tempted to do the wrong thing in your night dreams or daydreams, then get up and busy yourself in other ways. What pleases God? Seeking to please God instead of seeking to please ourselves and others pleases God! (Of course, we please God by seeking to *help* others, too.) Do not ever make the mistake that your struggles with unclean desires will end while you are on Earth. While you are on Earth, they will remain daily struggles — some days easier and some days more difficult.

Ultimately, we must be willing to forsake our carnal desires and willing to forsake pleasing all others in order to be a fitting companion for our Lord. In order to find our real Self, we must be willing to lose our false self as well as lose who we thought we were. Instead, we must try to remember who we were in God before our Fall from Him. (Metaphysically speaking, the Adamic Fall was more like a Crash.) It is in the application of the shed blood of God's only-begotten Son that permits such far memories to return. We need to arrive at the juncture where we can state with conviction: "I know who I am because I remember what I once was and now am again through the shed blood of God's only-begotten Son."

Here are the major steps necessary for you to please God:

1. Recognize continually that it is God who created you and not you yourself. If this is already self-evident to you, then you need to understand that it is not self-evident to everyone else. Satan believes that he created himself. Fallen angels and unclean spirits believe that they have created themselves. And human beings who are earthly power brokers believe that they are in the business of creating themselves.

2. Learn your vulnerabilities and know that they are ever-present with you while you are on Earth. Make a mental list of your vulnerabilities so that you can consolidate them into a mental check sheet. You may make a written list of your vulnerabilities but only to help you remember what they are. Destroy the written list as soon as it is finished, but only after you have first memorized it.

3. As temptations arise daily for you to entertain and indulge unclean desires related to your vulnerabilities, actively respond by thinking other thoughts and feeling other emotions, meditating on God's written Word, and busying yourself in activities that are neutral, harmless, and/or beneficial to you as well as to others in that they are pleasing to God.

4. When you slip up, as you invariably will, do not beat yourself up by accusing yourself or by misconcluding that you are guilty before God or condemned by Him. It is Satan's job to accuse the people of

God, not yours; besides, you should not be listening to Satan anyway because his accusations are false. Rather than allowing guilt and condemnation to grow within you, you should just allow your resolve to please God to grow even stronger.

Yes, seeking to please God pleases God. We do not need to be omniscient in order to please God. God understands that our personal referent is limited by our own corporeality, life experiences, and education or lack thereof. If truly pleasing God involves doing God's Will, then it is legitimate to ask: "What is God's Will?" Knowing God's Will involves understanding what God has to say to us through His Holy Bible, His Holy Spirit, His holy messengers, and which of our requests God chooses to honor or not honor. Sometimes we try to tell God what His Will is or what it should be. Without realizing it, we dishonor God through such arrogance.

To be sure, we should take custody of our thoughts, feelings, ideas, and imaginations. We should be able to present every one of them to God for His approval or disapproval.

Exercises and Activities in Christian Metaphysics

1. When we seek to please our Creator-God, how is it that we really end up pleasing ourselves and others?

2. Do we remain created beings eternally or do our souls get swallowed up by an invisible vortex of energy known as *God?* Please explain.

3. What might critics of Christian metaphysics use for their argument against its validity? What might they be failing to do?

4. How can our future bodies each have substance, tangibility, and a somatic identity and not be physical?

5. In the reality of God, who is "me" and "you" or "us" and "them"?

6. The problem with some "Word-of-faith" and "prosperity" movements is that, in effect, they *tell* God what to do. When we tell God what He should do, what are we lacking? (Answers to this question may vary.)

7. Considering your current character deficits, what will be your future major character strengths? When will that transformation take place?

8. How do we achieve our greatest goals? Please explain.

9. How do you plan to become a more fitting companion for your Creator-God? (Personalize the four major steps given in the text for you to please God.)

10. What does taking custody of your thoughts, feelings, ideas, and imagination mean for you personally?

Chapter Five

The Quest for Harmony

Genesis and the Natural Sciences

Authentic Christians who hold to the authority of the Holy Bible understand that if they encounter details, concepts, or facts in the Bible that seemingly contradict one another, and that if the seemingly contradictory details have not been artificially created by copyists, translators, and/or publishers who have added to or subtracted from the original text by mistake or their own misguided attempts to resolve such differences, then the inability to bridge gaps and reconcile differences between and among seemingly contradictory details, concepts, and facts must come from the students' own lack of understanding (all authentic Christians remain lifelong students of the Holy Bible).

In other words, real students of the Holy Bible accept personal responsibility for their own inability to bridge any gaps and/or reconcile any seeming differences in Scriptural details, concepts, or facts. To be sure, one cannot fully understand the Holy Bible unless one has accepted the Lord Jesus Christ as personal Savior as well as Savior of the world. Without such acceptance, we do not have God's Holy Spirit resident within us. And without God's Holy Spirit resident within us, we are lost when it comes to fully understanding the Holy Bible. The responsibility for fully understanding the Holy Bible is twofold: (1) God's Holy Spirit is responsible for unveiling the spiritual significance of the Holy Bible to us; and (2) we are responsible for regularly reading, rereading, and studying the Holy Bible with a strong desire to understand and a willingness to use other resources to help us understand.

Harmony, harmonize, and *harmonization* mean different things to different people. For various theology students and scholars of the Holy Bible, these words can also have several different meanings. *For example:* (1) some might use these words relative to correlating the events recorded within the four gospels; (2) some might use these words concerning written attempts to rearrange sections of the Holy Bible chronologically in order to make better sense of a complex and complicated sequence of events (like the Apostle Paul's journeys in relationship to his epistles); and (3) some might use the same words relative to any attempts at reconciling seemingly contradictory or complex details, concepts, and facts found in the Holy Bible.

For the purposes of this book, *harmony, harmonize,* and *harmonization* are used in general reference to resolving conflict between and among any details, concepts, or facts that seem to be at odds with one another regardless of source. The premise that failure to resolve such differences comes from a lack within our own understanding is very important to the objective of this section, which seeks to reconcile seeming differences between perspectives concerning the origin of life derived solely from the Genesis account and perspectives derived solely from the natural sciences.

Some spiritual concepts will forever remain illogical to people who rely mainly on deductive and inductive reasoning or on scientific principles for their own understanding of the meaning of life. *For example,* the concept of forgiveness without the expectation of something in return or without the purpose of benefiting one's own psychological well-being might be illogical to those who garner meaning to life, life experiences, and social interactions by relying mainly on (1) deductive and inductive reasoning or (2) scientific principles. Authentic Christians recognize that they can only understand the need for forgiveness spiritually, supernaturally, and metaphysically from their standpoint of faith in God through Jesus Christ. So, for them, there may be no need to harmonize the concept of such unsullied forgiveness with, say, the inability to forgive due to mental deficiencies, emotional inadequacies, or organic brain disorders. They recognize that the two (i.e., the ability to forgive and the inability to forgive) are difficult to reconcile and that harmony might not be possible and may not always be necessary regardless of how beneficial it might be for one's worldview. Although they might be able to attribute the lack of forgiveness to spiritual causes, they might not be able to reconcile (1) the existence of forgiveness through Christ's perfect love and (2) the inability to forgive due to organic deficiencies, inadequacies, or pathologies. However, it is our responsibility to harmonize such different views in order to be well-balanced, less judgmental, and growth-oriented.

Unfortunately, many people who believe in the authority of the Holy Bible do not see the necessity for harmonizing the Genesis account of creation with perspectives held to be true in the natural sciences. It is unfortunate because the seeming variances between the Genesis account and prevailing views in anthropology, archeology, astronomy, biology, chemistry, geology, and physics exist mainly because of the ways in which people have been taught to hold the views as irreconcilable. Many Christians are taught to fear evidence from the natural sciences or to believe in some ridiculous pseudo-science that attempts to validate perverted doctrinal perspectives and misguided religious conclusions. (In misguided religious conclusions, the cart always goes before the horse.) It is equally unfortunate that most natural scientists are taught to seek only natural explanations for all phenomena, including supernatural events and miracles; it is unfortunate because they ignore the possibility that some faith-based explanations may not only be valid but the only ones possible.

Since the Biblical account of creation indicates that the sun, moon, and stars were not created until the fourth *day*,[17] solar time, lunar time, and sidereal (or stellar) time did not exist to measure time for the first three so-called *days* of creation. The eisegesis[18] of conservative

---

[17] Genesis 1:14-19

[18] *Eisegesis* is defined here as "interpretation with personal, or subjective, bias."

theologians would argue that the Hebrew word for *day* always means a twenty-four hour period of time throughout the entire Holy Bible. They fail to take into consideration that there are places in the Holy Bible that state "one day with the Lord is as a thousand years, and a thousand years as one day"[19] and that the planet Earth during its formation had days that were much shorter than they are now. The rotation of the planet Earth about its axis has slowed down considerably since its formation (and it continues to slow down). The Earth's earliest days were closer to six hours in duration.

Conservative Christian theologians would also argue that the use of the words "morning" and "evening" for the first three days — recorded in Genesis 1:5, 1:8, and 1:13 — reinforces the notion that the *days* in the Genesis account were exactly as they are now. However, without solar, lunar, and stellar light during the first three *days* of creation, there could be no morning and evening as we understand them today. Therefore, either "morning" and "evening" are referring to different standards or they are included simply for the purpose of literary parallelism for each of the recorded seven *days* of creation, much like the parallelism found in the repeating fourteen generations in the genealogy of Jesus Christ that is recorded in Chapter One of the Gospel of Matthew. (That some generations have been omitted in Chapter One of Matthew is acknowledged by many conservative Christian theologians.)

Certainly, it is not impossible to reconcile the seven *days* of the Genesis account of creation with prevailing views in the natural sciences if one uses: (1) the concept of a "fast forward" presentation of creation events in Genesis; or (2) the concept that God can slow down or speed up time at His Will:

1. A "fast forward" perspective is a concept understood by many conservative Christian theologians — *for example,* in explaining the seventieth week of Daniel (Daniel 9:24-27), some scholars skip

---

[19] 2 Peter 3:8, King James Version (see also Psalm 90:4)

time and resume counting when relevant events begin again in the future. (I make this point not to endorse their view on the seventieth week but to indicate that the "fast forward" concept is embraced by people who are not labeled heretics by mainstream Christians.) Another example of a "fast forward" is found in between verses 23 and 24 in 1 Corinthians 15, where the Apostle Paul "fast forwards" 1,000 years from the time of Christ Jesus' return (verse 23) to the time that Christ Jesus delivers his kingdom to God the Father (verse 24).

2. That God can slow down or speed up time is a concept understood by many conservative Christian theologians — *for example,* when they acknowledge that God slowed down time to honor a request from Hezekiah, King of Judah (2 Kings 20:8-11).

The present author proposes that the inability to reconcile seemingly contradictory and/or complex details, concepts, and facts in the Genesis account of creation with prevailing views regarding astronomical, geologic, and biological events held in the natural sciences is due to a failure to think metaphysically.

For example, a metaphysical harmony could be achieved between the Genesis account of the creation of Adam and Eve and prevailing views in anthropology and astronomy if the Genesis account of the creation of Adam and Eve represents the original appearance of those two individuals in the Garden of Eden (an incorporeal Paradise) at the same time that the planet Earth already had a race of hominids (or *hominins,* depending on how taxonomically precise one desires to be) without souls. Such harmonization would posit that when Adam and Eve fell and were expelled from Paradise (an incorporeal state in eternity), they became "frozen" in the relative space-time of the material universe (a corporeal state). In other words, their appearance in corporeality, or human flesh, was coincident with, and dependent on, their fall from their original glorious estate in God's Paradise, the Garden of Eden. This would also help explain with whom their sons, Cain and Seth, mated. If the mates of Cain and Seth were hominids without souls, it would also make sense if their offspring were gifted with souls by God because of their descendancy from Adam and Eve through Cain and Seth.

It is very clear from the Holy Bible that Adam and Eve were individual people who lived *approximately* 6,000 years ago based on the genealogies carefully recorded throughout the Old Testament, or *Tanakh* (i.e., the Hebrew Bible). Of course, the genealogies in the Old Testament are tedious reading but necessary in order for us to calculate the *approximate* passage of time since the fall of Adam and Eve.

Whatever else the Holy Bible is or isn't, it is a book that primarily covers 7,000 years of Earth time: (1) 4,000 years from the appearance of Adam and Eve in corporeal flesh (i.e., at the time of their "Fall") to the first advent of Jesus Christ; (2) 2,000 years from the time of the first advent of Jesus Christ to the second advent of Jesus Christ; and (3) 1,000 years for the millennial reign of Jesus Christ on Earth, culminating in World War IV (the Battle of Gog and Magog), the Great White Throne Judgment of God, and the creation of "a new heaven and a new earth" (Revelation 20:8, 20:11, and 21:1). The majority of Christians and natural scientists should be able to agree on the chronological nature of the Holy Bible relative to this 7,000 year period of Earth time. If that is their starting point for mutual understanding and agreement, then the majority of the desired harmonization will have been accomplished already.

It is also very clear from the Holy Bible that, in addition to it being the name for an individual person, the name *Adam* is also a plural word that represents humanity as a whole, *Homo sapiens* in general, and an entire species of hominids. *Adam* is a Hebrew plural word for male and female corporeal beings with an iron-based, or *reddish,* pigment. (*Reddish* here is not referring directly to skin tone but to the hue of iron-containing oxygenated blood.)

The seeming differences between the Genesis account of creation and the facts and well-grounded theories of natural science can be reconciled with much harmony resulting *if:*

1. Christians and natural scientists would read Genesis 1:1 through Genesis 2:7 as a condensation, or capsulization, of astronomical, geologic, and biological events that includes the emergence of an entire species of hominids known as *Homo sapiens;*

2. Christians and natural scientists would read Genesis 2:8 through Genesis 2:25 as a description of the separate formation of a heavenly paradise known as the Garden of Eden and the separate creation of an incorporeal being named Adam with the accompanying metaphysical cloning of Eve from Adam (this, of course, presupposes that the Garden of Eden is in a parallel, incorporeal world superimposed over and above the planet Earth in a different plane of consciousness that has a heavenly, absolute, and eternal space-time); and

3. Christians and natural scientists would read Genesis 3:1 through Genesis 3:24 as a condensation, or capsulization, of the fall to temptation of the individual created beings known as Adam and Eve that resulted in their expulsion from a heavenly, absolute, and incorporeal state (i.e., the Garden of Eden, or "Paradise") to an earthly, or corporeal, state (i.e., the planet Earth).

Although physical coordinates are given in Genesis 2:10 through Genesis 2:14 for the Garden of Eden, those coordinates can be understood metaphysically as *also* representing a place in a parallel, incorporeal world superimposed over and above the planet Earth in a different plane of consciousness that has a heavenly space-time. This is the reason that Christ Jesus referred to the Kingdom of God as within us, right next to us, and beside us. This is also the reason that the heavenly paradise of God is also described as a garden with trees in Revelation 2:7, 22:2, and 22:14.

If you are *only* looking to find flaws in the present author's metaphysical harmonization of the Genesis account of creation and the facts and well-grounded theories on the origin of life from the natural sciences, then you are missing the major point he is trying to make. Regardless of whether the present author's harmonization is precisely correct or not, such harmonization should be attempted in order to show that the two bodies of knowledge (one body of knowledge supernatural and the other body of knowledge natural) can be complementary and not opposing.

Metaphysically speaking, are Christian people not *trans-species?* (Here, the present author is *not* writing about dysphoric people or contemporary pagan people sometimes referred to as *furries,* he is writing about fallen, albeit saved, created beings who feel like aliens on Earth because they know their home is in Heaven.) Are saved people not spiritual beings living in corporeal bodies? Are we not strangers in a strange land? Will we not leave our human bodies behind one day? Will saved fallen created beings not have new bodies, or refreshed somatic identities, that will be more representative of who we really are at the time of Christ's return to Earth? If you can agree with this, picture this, imagine this, and understand this, then you are thinking metaphysically. And if you can think metaphysically about the future that is described in the Holy Bible, then you should be able to think metaphysically about the ancient past that is described in Genesis as well.

Thinking Metaphysically

Anytime that you think beyond the physical, material, or corporeal realm or beyond physical activities associated with that realm, you are thinking metaphysically. Thinking metaphysically is thinking conceptually about what is hidden to our physical senses. Thinking metaphysically requires searching for a higher, greater, and invisible reality that can be experienced only through the heightened and elevated spiritual sense that is derived supernaturally from God's Holy Spirit.

If you construct a graph on paper using x, y, and z axes and can imagine how the graph would look three-dimensionally and you assign meaning to the graph, then you are thinking metaphysically. If physical objects represent concepts to you *(for example,* if an upholstered armchair represents relaxation to you), then you are thinking metaphysically. If you can think of interrelated concepts as intersecting geometric shapes *(for example,* as correlated factors represented by a Venn diagram), then you can think metaphysically. Thinking metaphysically is thinking outside of the box where the box was only an idea to begin with. Although quantification may not occur when you think metaphysically, qualification always does; you may not think in terms of numbers and percentages using quantities, but you will always think in terms of characteristics and descriptive aspects using qualities.

If you actually understand that the shed blood of Jesus Christ cleansed you of all iniquity and sin, then you are thinking metaphysically. If you believe that you are alive in Christ Jesus, then you are thinking metaphysically. If you look for spiritual reasons or causes to explain the situations and circumstances you are in, then you are thinking metaphysically. If you say "I see" when you finally understand a difficult concept, then you are expressing yourself metaphysically.

In order to clarify if they are thinking metaphysically or non-metaphysically, some people might begin their spoken and written thoughts with phrases like: "Metaphysically speaking," "Spiritually speaking," "Supernaturally speaking," "Humanly speaking," "Physically speaking," "Corporeally speaking," "From a metaphysical standpoint," "From a spiritual standpoint," "From a supernatural standpoint," "From a human standpoint," "From a fleshly standpoint," "From an earthly standpoint," "From a physical standpoint," "From a corporeal standpoint," or "From a natural standpoint."

People who think metaphysically might proclaim: (1) "My emotional, mental, physical, and spiritual stability, grounding, and security are in God!" (2) "I am already whole and complete in God through Christ Jesus!" And (3) "It is the Creator-God, and the Creator-God alone, who validates and affirms my selfhood, being, and experience!"

If you believe that you are whole and healthy in Christ Jesus regardless of your physical condition, then you are applying metaphysical principles to your daily life. If you are a Christian who happens to be paraplegic and you claim that you walk daily with the Lord Jesus Christ and that you are running a race to please God, then you are looking beyond appearances to a higher reality that is metaphysical, and not physical, in nature.

One of the reasons to study Christian metaphysics is to help us separate legitimate spiritual thinking from thinking steeped in superstition and mythology. Thinking about the omniscience, omnipotence, and omnipresence of the invisible Creator-God always involves metaphysical thinking. Yes, God came to Earth in the form of Jesus Christ, but He came to help us understand eternal truths and to present Himself to us in a more relatable way. Additionally, God came to us in flesh as God the Son to teach us the difference between what has real value and what has no value at all, what pleases the Creator-God and what displeases the Creator-God, and how to behave and how not to behave. Jesus Christ is our eternal role model and our eternal mentor through God's Holy Spirit. Of course, first and foremost, *God the Son* gave his life for us as the only substitutionary offering acceptable to *God the Father* for our iniquity and sin. Salvation-in-itself through Jesus Christ can only be understood metaphysically. We must be careful not to assign superstitious and mythological value to salvation. We must believe, but we must understand what we believe and know why we believe it.

Thinking metaphysically goes way beyond thinking in figurative or poetic language and only using one's imagination in intellectual or academic pursuits. For Christians, thinking metaphysically requires: (1) an imagination that is tethered to God by His Holy Spirit; (2) looking for and applying general spiritual truths and principles to daily living; and (3) expressing our thoughts in language that seeks to keep our own consciousness elevated at the same time that it seeks to elevate the consciousness of others.

Thinking metaphysically does not mean that you are so Heaven bound that you are no earthly good. It does not mean that you are so lost in thought that you shirk your daily responsibilities and duties. It does not mean that you use poetic language to impress others or to puff up the image you have of yourself. It does not mean that you play "word police" or "thought police" in order to fix, or correct, the colloquial speech or individual thinking of others so that it does not suggest negativity. Instead, thinking metaphysically allows you to see that everyone is on their own personal journey and that we can share the spiritual concepts and ideas to which we subscribe with each other in a calm, courteous, and reasonable manner, looking to (1) keep the concepts that resonate within our souls and are complementary to Biblical principles and (2) discard the concepts that are harmful or not helpful to us or are against God's absolute truth.

Thinking metaphysically includes recognizing that life is incorporeal before it is corporeal and that we were created as spiritual beings first. Thinking metaphysically enables you to catch a glimpse of the truth here and there, reminding yourself at the same time that, in corporeality, we only see and know in part. It helps you to realize that, although God is everywhere, He is not to be found in physical objects. It causes you to think of the sun, moon, planets, stars, solar systems, galaxies, and physical universe as representative of concepts, principles, and ideas in the mind of God. Metaphysical thinking even permits you to conceive of parallel universes existing side by side.

If you see a butterfly and can imagine that it represents a flying flower in God's spiritual universe, then you can think metaphysically. If you can look at water as a physical representation of God's Holy Spirit, then you can think metaphysically. If you can conceive that human images mask our compound, composite, collective, and corporate identities in Jesus Christ, then you can think metaphysically.

When you learn a spiritual principle, you are actually learning it metaphysically and if you try to practically apply it to relevant situations and conditions, then you are seeking to apply it metaphysically. When you think metaphysically, you understand that you are on a spiritual journey and that you are either moving toward or away from the Creator-God. Thinking metaphysically for human beings requires us to use earthly tools like alphabet letters, words, and sentences, but we should also be reminded that written language originated as pictographs and ideograms. Thus, thinking metaphysically requires us to think in pictures and ideas along with using contemporary alphabetic language.

Thinking metaphysically includes the recognition that spiritual principles build upon one another and that, once we learn one major spiritual principle, we are then better prepared to learn the next one. Thinking metaphysically requires refinement throughout one's life lived in spiritual inquiry combined with one's gratitude to God for everything that we have and all that we are. Thinking metaphysically enables us to select important concepts from the belief systems of others and accommodate and assimilate them into our own belief systems.

If you regularly look for an invisible reality behind the physical appearances that you see, then you are thinking metaphysically. If you acknowledge that there is a hidden, invisible reality behind the motives of others, then you are thinking metaphysically. If you understand that evil masquerades itself as good and that you may be fooled by evil, then you are thinking metaphysically. If you ask God to refine your ability to discern elements of His supernatural reality, then you are seeking to understand life metaphysically.

When you think metaphysically, you gradually become more aware of the cold, dead images that come from Satan's mortal mind and the crisp, animated images that come from God's divine Mind.

You cannot think of the Lord God Almighty without thinking metaphysically, but thinking metaphysically requires spiritual nurture and daily practice in thought, in mind, in word, and in deed.

Resolving Problems Metaphysically

Thinking metaphysically is a prelude to resolving problems metaphysically. Resolving problems metaphysically does not mean that you should not consult with employment agencies, marital counselors, educators, financial advisors, clergy, medical doctors, and therapists in order to help resolve your problems. No, resolving your problems with principles from Christian metaphysics means that you must seek to understand your problems and their solutions spiritually by recognizing and realizing that many of your problems and their solutions are beyond the scope of physicality, materiality, or corporeality. To be sure, this may seem enigmatic to you because most of your problems and their solutions manifest in physicality, materiality, or corporeality; thus, it is easy for you to conclude that their causes as well as their solutions must be entirely physical, material, or corporeal. You should not underestimate Christian metaphysics to help diagnose and treat a condition or situation that is problematic. However, in addition to never underestimating Christian metaphysics, you should never overestimate it either:

For example, you would never use Christian metaphysics alone to diagnose and treat a compound bone fracture when x-rays and titanium pins are necessary for resetting the bone to ensure its correct alignment in healing; and you would never use Christian metaphysics to diagnose and treat severe dehydration when the administration and monitoring of intravenous fluids provides the easiest, fastest, and safest way to replenish a dehydrated body's fluid compartments. You can *always* use Christian metaphysics *side by side* with other avenues for diagnosing a problem and formulating a solution to it. Of course, some Christians who desire to rely on prayer and God alone will take issue with this perspective. However, it is not the present author's desire to think for them or require them to think exactly like him or each other.

Here are some provisos for the contemporary use of Christian metaphysics:

1. Christian metaphysics for the third millennium of the Christian era is a way of looking at life that recognizes and acknowledges the existence of a supernatural reality and a spiritual universe in addition to the existence of a corporeal reality and a physical universe. However, contemporary Christian metaphysics employs the understanding that a supernatural reality and its accompanying spiritual universe supersede any and all physical, material, or corporeal realities without denigrating the practicality of physical, material, or corporeal solutions to physical, material, or corporeal problems.

2. Employing Christian metaphysics during the third millennium of the Christian era does not mean pitting it against the best practices of medicine, psychology, or other established healing arts; rather, it means seeking to complement, enhance, and work alongside those practices.

3. Christian metaphysics for the third millennium of the Christian era does not do away with relying radically on God for healing to the exclusion of all other practices. It just includes the recognition that employing such reliance varies based on time, place, condition, and situation. To be sure, we are always to trust in God completely for all healing, but Christian metaphysics for the third millennium includes the understanding that God works, at times, not only in mysterious ways but also in different ways for different conditions in different people in order to address mental, emotional, physical, and spiritual healing not in just one individual but in us all collectively and corporately.

4. Christian metaphysics for the third millennium of the Christian era includes the understanding that multiple variables are involved in human conditions and, for that reason alone, men and women with God-given intelligence try to use all that God has revealed to humanity through His goodness.

5. Christian metaphysics for the third millennium of the Christian era is completely compatible with Biblical Christianity and the millennial rule of Jesus Christ on Earth.

6. In their application of divine healing principles, authentic practitioners of Christian metaphysics during the third millennium of the Christian era always defer to the sovereignty of Jesus Christ and the supremacy of God's absolute truth. In other words, authentic practitioners of Christian metaphysics *never* assume that they know everything there is to know about diagnosing a particular problem and treating it.

7. All practitioners of Christian metaphysics during the third millennium of the Christian era seek to harmonize the principles they use with the efficacy of other practices that are within the supreme and sovereign Will of God.

Following are examples of how to help resolve problems using Christian metaphysics:

Unemployment and Underemployment

In addition to education and training to prepare oneself for a job as well as using a regular and systematic approach to finding a job, job seekers can employ principles of Christian metaphysics to be led to a job and gain confidence in finding a job, interviewing for a job, and even performing well while employed at a job. In order to use principles of Christian metaphysics to treat unemployment and underemployment, we must first confess that the Lord Jesus Christ is in control of everything. Then, we must seek to understand what it means that God always provides for His people along with the understanding that God does not always provide for His people in ways that we think He should or in accordance with our personal timelines.

With that said, we also need to recognize and declare that, in God, we are already employed to carry out His Will — provided, of course, that we are approaching the Creator-God in humility and gratitude. We should also look at the following as actions of faith rather than necessary evils: constructing résumés, sending out query letters, filling out job applications, using employment agencies, travelling to potential job sites, and practicing answers to potential questions in job interviews. We need to employ the knowledge that, although we may not see the light at the end of the tunnel, the light is always there.

To use Christian metaphysics practically, we must recognize that, first and foremost, employment is always spiritual. And we must pray that God will open doors for us, cause us to find favor with others, and lead us to the right place at the right time. If we cannot find specific employment, then we must pray that God grant us the creativity to develop new ideas and products that are useful, marketable, and salable to others.

Spousal Difficulties

In addition to premarital and marital counseling from credible and reputable specialists, spouses who seek to improve their relationships can use principles of Christian metaphysics to approach and resolve spousal difficulties spiritually. In order to use principles of Christian metaphysics to treat marital problems, we must first confess that the Lord Jesus Christ is in control of everything. We must also not blame God for what we have chosen to do without His counsel and consent. If we have permitted someone else to select a spouse for us, or have personally chosen criteria that limit our selection of a spouse, then we must not later accuse God of bringing the wrong person into our lives. We must also recognize that, although certain cultural and personal values are important to honor, it is more important to honor the leading of God's Holy Spirit in selecting a companion.

Sometimes God provides us with a companion that we reject. We are in error whenever we choose to accomplish our own will rather than

God's Will. We can never achieve our greatest goals if we choose to do things alone (i.e., without seeking God's counsel first and honoring that counsel). If the truth be told, we are already married to God through the shed blood of Jesus Christ (i.e., we are in a covenant partnership with the Lord God Almighty). In other words, regardless of whether we are male or female, we are already *Mrs. Jesus.* Individually, collectively, and corporately, we are the Companion of our Creator-God.

Applying principles of Christian metaphysics to spousal problems helps us to recognize that most problems come from a battle of individual human wills, perspectives, and opinions. So, we need to put our individual wills, perspectives, and opinions down to pick up the Will of God, to pick up our hands to pray that we see more clearly the spousal issues at hand and their resolutions, and to pick up our desire to please God through our words and deeds. God hates all forms of adultery — mental, emotional, and spiritual adultery in addition to sexual, or physical, adultery — because God loves our honor, commitment, and faithfulness not only to Him but also to each other. Do not blaspheme God's Holy Name by making false promises to Him; and do not weaken a spousal relationship by making promises that you cannot keep, will not keep, or never had the intention of keeping.

Apply to your relationships the principle of Christian metaphysics that you should never let yourself be treated as less than you are because, in the final analysis, you are as you see yourselves. Never grant authority to emotional, mental, physical, religious, or spiritual abuse either in yourself or in others. If you indulge such parasitic thinking, you are not spiritually mature enough for a successful spousal relationship and you will have destined yourself to do things alone.

Finally, also apply the principle of Christian metaphysics that, because our Creator-God is the God of resurrection, He can resurrect relationships that have been spoiled because of battling wills, perspectives, and opinions. Our God can harmonize our communications with one another by seeing to it that our thoughts and feelings are conveyed and received in the best ways possible.

Preparing for your Future

Although God's Holy Spirit is the teacher of all spiritual truth, we must be better prepared to live in this world by learning: (1) an alphabet; (2) words; (3) the definitions of words; (4) the subtle meanings, or nuances, of words (their semantics); (5) how to use words properly in sentences (their syntax, or word placement); and (6) how to string sentences together to demonstrate well-grounded, well-reasoned, and cohesive thinking. We must also be willing to learn a body of knowledge that has practicality for ourselves and others. However, in order for all of what we learn to be important and have purpose for ourselves and others, we must dedicate our lives in honor of our Creator-God. Everything we say and do must first be offered up to God for His approval.

In order to use principles of Christian metaphysics to receive the best education and training possible, we must first confess that the Lord Jesus Christ is in control of everything. Then, we must seek to understand what education and training mean in the context of pleasing God and helping others individually and society as a whole. With that said, we also need to recognize and declare that God provides for His people by creating opportunities for them to receive the appropriate education and training that are complementary to the spiritual gifts He has given to them. To use Christian metaphysics practically, we must seek education and training from reputable and credible mentors, educators, trainers, and advisors at the same time that we recognize and declare that it is God Himself who provides for our education and training and who creates opportunities for us to learn, and be trained to do, what pleases Him by helping others in His Name.

Ask God what you should do in your life. Don't tell Him. Always declare His goodness despite the difficulties of learning to do what is useful and pleasing to God at the same time that it is useful and pleasing to yourself and others.

Solving Financial Problems

In order to use principles of Christian metaphysics to solve financial problems, we must first confess that the Lord Jesus Christ is in control of everything. To use principles of Christian metaphysics concerning finances, we must also remember that God has given to us all that we already have. So, although we may have used substantial personal effort during difficult times, we must remember to give God all of the glory, honor, and praise for what has been accomplished, earned, and achieved through Him. If we only have access to one commodity, then we should be thankful that we have it. If we lose access to that one commodity, then we should be thankful that we never need to worry about losing it again. The point here is that we must always start with gratitude for what we have even if it *appears* that we have nothing.

Always look for something to be grateful for. Contradict worry about insufficiency, anxiety about inadequacy, and fear of loss by grasping tightly the metaphysical principle that God is always in control and that God always provides for His people. Let us raise a banner of gratitude to our Lord and never let it down for what we already have and for what we will have one day in Heaven.

Financial currency has extrinsic value but its value does not approach the intrinsic metaphysical value of God's love, grace, mercy, forgiveness, and the impartation of His Holy Spirit to us. God's love, grace, mercy, forgiveness, and Holy Spirit constitute the only real currencies that can be exchanged between and among us all. These currencies possess real tangibility and are truly substantive. If we seek to find and use these currencies, all things will come together and we will not only be grateful for, but also satisfied with, what we have now, what we will have tomorrow, and what we will have throughout eternity.

Losing our Religion

In order to use principles of Christian metaphysics to counter intensely negative views on religion, we must first confess that the Lord Jesus Christ is in control of everything and that His religion is a religion of service and not a religious service.

Religion is not a bad word. Metaphysically speaking, *religion* is the practice of our faith in God by helping others in the name of our Lord and Savior, Jesus Christ. To be truly religious means that we regularly practice our faith by helping others and seeing to the needs of others who suffer deprivation and who might not be able to help themselves. To practice our faith includes using the strength and resources that God has given to us to share with those who are in a weakened, or infirm, state and who may be experiencing debilitating emotional difficulties in their lives.

God sees religion metaphysically. We should, too. We cannot lose our religion if we remember that our purpose in life is to please God by helping others as we testify of the love of our Savior, Jesus Christ. Helping others in the name of Jesus Christ is non-liturgical religion. Indeed, such help has real mass importance.

Biblia Apotheka

The present author's coined phrase *Biblia Apotheka* means "Word-based pharmacy." The phrase includes the English transliteration of the Greek word for "books" (meaning "the Bible" or "God's written Word") and an English transliteration of the Greek word for "storehouse" or "barn" — from which the modern concept of a *pharmacy* is derived. The Holy Bible is a storehouse that contains spiritual medicine for the soul; in that way, it is a "Word-based pharmacy." People who use Christian metaphysics look in the Holy Bible for prescriptions to treat what ails them.

To be sure, in order to use principles of Christian metaphysics to treat life's problems, we must first confess that the Lord Jesus Christ is in control of everything. At the same time, people who use Christian metaphysics for the purpose of treating life's problems know that many physical, material, or corporeal conditions can be traced back to their spiritual roots, which are the moral weaknesses and spiritual infirmities within us personally.

To be sure, carnal mind is the intellect of the animal, abased, or lower self that is played upon, and preyed upon, by Satan's mortal mind, but the tempting thoughts, feelings, images, ideas, and scenarios that are woven into our imaginations by Satan's mortal mind can only speak to us if we have the propensity to indulge them — or, in other words, only if we already have the moral weakness or spiritual infirmity that can be influenced by the specific images and scenarios projected onto our imaginations from Satan's mortal mind. For this reason, whenever we sense an attack by Satan's mortal mind through the carnal mind of our lower, abased, or animal self, we must immediately take our infirmity or weakness and lay it at the feet of our Lord and Savior, Jesus Christ. We do this by confessing it (i.e., presenting it) to God as fast as we can. As we mature spiritually, we do this spontaneously without needing to think about it or make a decision to do so; in other words, it becomes a metaphysical knee-jerk reaction for us. As soon as we recognize that we are in a state of temptation, we need to go home physically and metaphysically. For the sake of clarification, the metaphysical definition of *home* is "wherever God is."

Satan's mortal mind appeals to our misguided desires for self-aggrandizement that seek to compensate for our feelings of inadequacy and low self-esteem. Such desires and feelings in saved people are vestiges from the Adamic Fall, when we were first separated from our Creator-God. When saved people tap into their higher self, supraself, or absolute identity in God, these desires and feelings dissipate and disappear.

As a side note here, to avoid the risk of concluding that Satan's mortal mind only attacks us through visual-type images and scenarios in our imaginations, it is important to understand that Satan's mortal mind also tries to tempt us by stimulating auditory hallucinations in our imaginations as well. When this happens, Satan's mortal mind uses suggestive words, phrases, and word plays in the hope of evoking visual-type images and scenarios in our imaginations that lead us into temptation. Sometimes, Satan's mortal mind will even use our own words and phrases to help gain access to our souls. For this reason, it is important that we are careful not to use derisive humor against any one of God's created beings regardless of whether they are fallen or unfallen or whether they are saved or unsaved. Just as we do not play with unclean spirits, so do we not play with unclean thoughts, unclean feelings, unclean visual images, and unclean words (i.e., words that are hurtful or represent unclean things and activities).

In spiritual maturity, we eventually recognize that visual-type and auditory-type Satanic attacks will continue daily and our appropriate responses are required daily for as long as we live in the earth plane of consciousness. For this reason, we learn spiritual hypervigilance as our defense in Christ Jesus. With strength and power from God's Holy Spirit through the shed blood of Christ Jesus, mature people of God never tire or become despondent. Spiritually mature people never think "Have I not overcome this already?" because they know that the invisible attacks of the Enemy are unrelenting. Then, let us remember daily that it is the nature of Satan's mortal mind to be unrelenting. We should also never take it personally by misconcluding that such attacks make us dirty or separate us from God, our universal Self, because there is no doubt that God is really our heavenly Dad (true moms and dads always stick close to their children no matter how badly they mess up).

Let us never open a door or window to unclean desires in the fortress-home that God has given to us through Christ Jesus.

Exercises and Activities in Christian Metaphysics

1. How is responsibility for understanding the Holy Bible twofold?

2. Using external resources, investigate the theological meaning of *harmony, harmonize,* and *harmonization* as they relate to a study of the Holy Bible. Briefly describe the meaning of these three words theologically.

3. Whose responsibility is it to harmonize the Genesis account of creation with facts and well-grounded theories in the natural sciences?

4. What is the difference between *exegesis* and *eisegesis?*

5. Draw a simple timeline for the 7,000 years of continuous time that the Holy Bible covers and use the following phrases to label major events and timeframes: *the Fall of Adam and Eve, birth of Christ Jesus, death of Christ Jesus, the Church Age, the Tribulation, the return of Christ Jesus, the Millennium of Peace, World War IV (the Battle of Gog and Magog), the Great White Throne Judgment of God,* and *the creation of "a new heaven and a new earth."*

6. Name one benefit from trying to harmonize the Genesis account of creation and the facts and well-grounded theories on the origin of life from the natural sciences.

7. In your own words, what does it mean to *think metaphysically?*

8. Give at least three examples of how you think metaphysically.

9. What are the three requirements for thinking metaphysically?

10. How can we reconcile using contemporary language with thinking metaphysically?

11. Give at least one example of underestimating Christian metaphysics and at least one example of overestimating Christian metaphysics.

12. In one paragraph, summarize the seven provisos for the contemporary use of Christian metaphysics.

13. Briefly discuss how you personally can use Christian metaphysics to help during periods of unemployment or underemployment.

14. Briefly discuss how you personally can use Christian metaphysics to help you find a spouse or improve a spousal relationship.

15. Briefly discuss how you personally can use Christian metaphysics to help you better prepare for your future.

16. Briefly discuss how you personally can use Christian metaphysics to help you solve financial problems.

17. Briefly discuss how you can use principles of Christian metaphysics to help others who might have intensely negative views on religion.

18. What should you do as soon as you recognize that you are in a state of temptation? Please explain.

Chapter Six

The Will of Our Universal Self

The Supremacy and Sovereignty of God's Will

Before God created us, God knew that newly-created beings with volition would be tempted to use their freedom by disobeying His Will. God always knows the end before the beginning and all outcomes even before their causes occur. Despite this knowledge, God created us anyway. God also knew that, despite our stepping outside of His Will, many of us would eventually step back into His Will given the opportunity to do so, thereby renewing a bond between Creator and created that would never again be threatened or broken. Permitting our fall to temptation was God's way of testing, trying, and teaching created beings in order for us to learn the eternal value of abiding (i.e., walking and communing) with God in the most intimate of ways.

Since we fell to temptation, does that mean we were flawed when we were created? No, we were only inexperienced. Inexperience is not a flaw. God did not create volitional beings with experience, bogus far memories, or preprogrammed decision-making abilities because that would have nullified His gift of individual free will to His newly-created souls. God does not make automatons, robots, or monsters. Only Satan does that.

During our lives on Earth, there comes a time when each soul consciously chooses to put either God's Will first or its own will first. When we choose to put God's Will first, it means that we have decided to seek to please God in all possible situations and circumstances. (Of course, we fail regularly.) As soon as we choose to put God first, God again becomes our universal Self. However, regardless of our instantaneous salvation upon our acceptance of Christ Jesus as our personal Savior, the process of God becoming our universal Self entirely and wholly is gradual. The process is gradual because it takes us time to learn to put His Will before our own will in every aspect of our human experience.

The prayer to our heavenly Father taught by Christ Jesus contains the sentence: "Your Will be done on Earth as it is in Heaven." This sentence is every bit as much a declaration of our submission to God's Will as it is a request for God to bring all things on Earth into line with His supreme and sovereign Will.

Our God's supreme and sovereign Will is always in operation in His spiritual universe. And our God's supreme and sovereign Will is always in operation in His physical universe — *for example,* concerning phenomena associated with thermodynamics, quantum mechanics, gravitation, and interactions governed by general and special relativity. Of course, God's supreme and sovereign Will is always in operation in the supernatural miracles that occur in His physical universe, too. However, our God's supreme and sovereign Will is not yet always in operation within the souls of fallen, albeit saved, created beings.

The woes on this Earth are caused primarily by humanity's disobedience to God's Will and not by chance. In fact, most natural disasters result from our *collective* disobedience to God's Will. Although these woes may seem to involve nonparticipants in the disobedience that is related to a specific woe, all adult people are indirectly involved if they remain silent about the disobedience and, thereby, acquiesce to its presence. Without God's protection, humanity would have (and should have) already annihilated itself long ago due to metaphysical reverberations from disobedience to the supreme and sovereign Will of God.

Metaphysically speaking, the stability of the fabric of the physical universe is directly related to the spiritual stability of souls in dust and their choosing to exalt God's divine Mind or Satan's mortal mind. This

112

goes way beyond the melting of polar ice caps in relationship to global warming from the excessive burning of hydrocarbons and resultant ozone depletion. When human beings blatantly disregard the Will of God, there is an increase in the release of kinetic energy from potential energy — *for example,* in between our Earth's tectonic plates as well as within the solar flares from our sun's corona. The increase in movement of the Earth's tectonic plates results in an increase in the intensity and number of earthquakes, tsunami waves, and volcanoes. And an increase in the number and intensity of coronal mass ejections (CMEs) impacts the Earth's atmospheric pressure and temperature gradients, contributing to climate change as well as an increase in the size and intensity of hurricanes, typhoons, and cyclones. To be sure, there is a ripple effect throughout our entire solar system from negative spiritual energy that stimulates the production and release of kinetic energy from potential energy (including nuclear "potential" energy in our sun).

Potential energy can be converted to kinetic energy by spiritual means in beneficial as well as harmful ways. Prayer, "laying on of hands," and positive thinking *(for example,* through love, gratitude, and humility) all have beneficial effects on the human body by generating a flux in electromagnetic currents that is healing in nature. In contrast, psychic attacks, emotional abuse, and negative thinking *(for example,* through hatred, ingratitude, and false pride) all have harmful effects on the human body by generating a flux in electromagnetic currents that is debilitating in nature.

Understanding the physical universe metaphysically requires looking beyond the events and changes that occur in order to identify their spiritual significance, meaning, and cause. Because the present author often speaks and writes of the spiritual universe and physical universe separately for the sake of discussion, it might be misconcluded that he means that they are completely separate when in fact there are interrelationships and interactions between the two.

Similarly, understanding the human body metaphysically requires looking beyond the events and changes that occur in it in order to identify their spiritual significance, meaning, and cause. Because the present author often speaks and writes of the fleshly body in contrast to the electromagnetic, or spirit, body for the sake of discussion, it also might be misconcluded that he means that they are completely separate when in fact there are interrelationships and interactions between the two for each human being.

Metaphysical thinking is the only thinking that helps to bridge the gap in our understanding between the physical universe and spiritual universe as well as between the human body and its electromagnetic, or spirit, body.

When the Will of God's divine Mind becomes our own collective will, there is a continuous flow of positive energy from the spiritual universe to the physical universe. And when the Will of God's divine Mind becomes our own personal will, there is a continuous flow of positive energy from our higher self, supraself, and absolute identity in God to our human, composite, and conscious functioning self.

Of course, the opposite is also true: When the will of Satan's mortal mind becomes our own collective will, the physical universe is impacted negatively. And when the will of Satan's mortal mind becomes our own personal will, our individual human, composite, and conscious functioning self is impacted negatively.

Lucifer fell when a desire to compete with the Creator-God developed within him. Because he sought to place his will above the Will of the Creator-God, Lucifer became the eternal Enemy of God (i.e., Adversary or Satan). Then, the angels that chose to imitate Lucifer were pulled into his downward spiral of evil dominance, domination, and dominion. Finally, God's newly-created, volitional beings — collectively known as Man (the upper case letter used here to denote a spiritually-corporate state of being in contrast to the corporeal state of being that exists for humanity) — fell because a desire to compete with God developed within them, too. How did this desire to compete manifest for Adam and Eve? They acted on Satan's temptation to place their individual wills above the Will of the Creator-God.

In summary, all created beings fall when our individual wills are in competition with the Will of the Creator-God. And, in the case of Man, created beings stay fallen until their individual wills are again yielded to, subsumed within, and subdued by the Will of God. However, there is no possibility for Satan, his fallen angels, or his unclean spirits to be returned to the Will of God because they are eternally damned. They blasphemed against God's Holy Spirit. Consequently, they are not only jealous of the Creator-God, they are also jealous of human beings because human beings have an opportunity for restoration through eternal redemption.

Competition with the Will of the Creator-God is an evil perversion of free will. Because competition makes sense to the animal, abased, and lower self, human beings misconclude that competition is necessary for survival when, in the spiritual reality of God, submission to His Will is what true survival is all about. Indeed, submitting our individual wills to the Will of God enables us to not only survive but flourish.

The carnal mind of the animal, abased, and lower self is *forever* in conflict with the Will of God. Satan's mortal mind is *forever* in conflict with the Will of God.[20] Carnal mind and Satan's mortal mind will one day no longer be factors that influence saved fallen created beings. However, until Satan's mortal mind is eternally condemned to the Lake of Fire along with all fallen angels and all unclean spirits, and carnal mind ceases with the dissolution of all corporeality, inner conflict will continue within all saved fallen created beings as well as unsaved fallen created beings who have not already handed themselves over completely to Satan's mortal mind.

---

[20] As used in this work, the word "forever" refers to a duration of time that is sustained only while corporeality continues to exist; and "eternity," "eternal," and "eternally" refer to the timeless state and place where the Creator-God, His unfallen created beings, and His saved created beings individually, collectively, and corporately live, move, and have their being.

For the sake of clarification, all saved created beings who have gone on to be with God in Heaven are no longer fallen and they no longer have inner conflict. All conflict ends instantaneously for saved fallen created beings the moment that they transition from a corporeal state to an incorporeal state (i.e., from being saints on Earth to being saints in Heaven). The possibility for change in conflict in unsaved fallen created beings depends on whether they are in an incarnate or discarnate state. If in an incarnate state, they must accept the shed blood of Jesus Christ as the only atonement acceptable to God the Father as payment for their iniquity and sin; then, they will be saved fallen created beings who await all inner conflict to cease at the time they go on to be with God in Heaven. If unsaved fallen created beings are in a discarnate state, they must wait to return to Earth in an incarnate state for any permanent change to take place. Why? God's spiritual law requires that a soul's acceptance of salvation must occur in an incarnate, and not a discarnate, state of being.

Conflict between and among human beings can be traced back to everyone trying to control each other by forcing their individual and group wills upon one another. All fallen created beings seek to rule and dominate each other. All conflict is a contest and a test of wills, including the conflict that exists between the Creator-God and Satan, between nations on Earth, between employer and employee, between co-workers, between friends, and between spouses. (This is not an exhaustive list.) In many instances, even pursuing someone else for the purpose of sexual intimacy is a matter of the pursuer trying to force his or her will upon the pursued, especially in terms of time and place. All fallen beings — including Satan, his angels, and his unclean spirits, and including human beings — are seeking to force their individual and collective wills upon others. (The word "force" here includes attempts to cunningly, craftily, and subtly manipulate others without their being aware.) Sooner or later, saved human beings learn to cease forcing their individual and collective wills on others. God, all unfallen angels, and all saved souls already in Heaven do not seek to exercise control over others because they share the same will, which is the Will of God, their universal Self. There is no competition in heaven today; there is only cooperation. The reason that the present author has written "today" in the previous sentence is because Satan and his fallen angels have already been booted out of Heaven, specifically at the time of Christ's crucifixion.

Most anger directed toward others is engendered in people because they perceive that their will has not been honored, obeyed, or respected. (This is not meant to imply that someone's will is worthy of being honored, obeyed, or respected over that of another.) The individual human will is a perversion of the free will exercised in created beings untainted by iniquity and sin. Free will in untainted individuals is cooperative and not competitive. Free will among such untarnished beings is hallmarked by mutual love, respect, and honor in obedience to the supreme and sovereign Will of God. As fallen, albeit saved, human beings, we are still learning to remove the tarnish from ourselves by yielding every aspect of our human will to the supreme and sovereign Will of God.

What should be our greatest desire?

Our greatest desire, individually and collectively, should be to show God our love by seeking to live, move, and have our being solely within His Will. (In other words, our greatest desire should be to please God.)

How can we achieve what should be our greatest desire?

We can achieve what should be our greatest desire, first and foremost, by becoming aware of what we do and why we do what we do, and, second, by putting each willful desire under the feet of Jesus Christ, our Lord and Savior. We need to acknowledge that all of our lusts are willful — that is, outside of the Will of God. We need to recognize that evaluating the worth and value of others using our own personality traits, the way we think, and how we individually respond and react to various situations and circumstances is willful because it is not within God's Will for us to do so. Willfulness includes placing our own individual and collective wills above the free will of other created beings and above the Will of God. All willfulness is unclean and

117

ungodly. Thus, we can only achieve what should be our greatest desire by carefully examining our every thought, our every feeling, our every word, our every imagined activity, and our every accomplished action to see if each is within the Will of God, our universal Self.

Satan, his fallen angels, his unclean spirits, and human beings who have committed the ultimate blasphemy against God's Holy Spirit are all beyond reclamation because they are eternally outside the Will of God. The Creator-God is not, and never will be, their universal Self. In fact, their self is not universal. Because their self was bloated, it imploded to become a spiritually-enblackened hole. Thus, the collective self of unclean entities has no identity other than in a perverted, sick, and sinful mass consciousness. The eternally damned are out of their minds in self-absorbed thinking, feeling, and frenzied activity. They shriek, groan, and cry out within a vacuum of dense darkness. They cannot be heard by those who are bathed in heavenly light. They have no hope and never will have any.

When we enter into a state of temptation, we place ourselves in danger. We misinterpret reality to be what it is not. We walk in a displaced state of mind that is outside of the supreme and sovereign Will of God. And we attract demonic beings who influence and compound our sinful thoughts, feelings, desires, and imaginations.

Lucifer's declarations against the Creator-God include the stated "I will!" as well as the implied "I will not!" The sin of Moses during the wilderness journey had him proudly declaring to the children of Israel: "I will do this for you!" rather than "God will continue to provide for you!" Judas Iscariot, the one-time Apostle, sought that his own will be done rather than the Will of God. Let us work daily by watching and praying to avoid such willfulness within ourselves. And let us thrill our Creator by obeying His Will, which is always supreme and sovereign.

How wonderful it is to live within the Will of God, our universal Self!

How to Combat Satan's Mortal Mind

Because Satan's mortal mind is insidiously deceptive, we must be living a certain life and lifestyle in our Lord Jesus Christ in order to be able to successfully combat it. The life and lifestyle that we live must be holy and pure. You might respond: "Well, that is impossible!" But it is not impossible because "we can do all things through Christ Jesus who strengthens us" (Philippians 4:13 KJV Paraphrase). Indeed, Christ Jesus is our strength. Christ Jesus is our power. In fact, we have no power apart from him.

Desiring to live a life of holiness and purity must be foremost in our minds if we are to successfully combat Satan's mortal mind. Yes, we will mess up periodically by missing the mark. However, as long as we are quick to confess our sins as well as the sinful thoughts, feelings, ideas, words, images, and scenarios that we entertain and indulge in our imaginations, we will not fall permanent victims to Satan's mortal mind. Oh, Satan's mortal mind will accuse us of justifiably opening ourselves up to demonic attack because of what we have confessed to God, but we must not believe these accusations because they are all lies. Satan's mortal mind tries to get us to believe lies so that we elect not to apply the shed blood of Jesus Christ to the situation or condition at hand. Grappling with Satan's mortal mind, some people misconclude that they are too far removed from the Creator-God to pray, meditate, and declare God's truth effectively.

In order to successfully combat Satan's mortal mind, it is imperative that we are honest with ourselves and with God. We must admit that something sinful is attractive to us, and we must confess as soon as a spirit of lust for power, wealth, possessions, position, title, or illicit sex overshadows us and before we enter a state of being that is even more difficult to overcome because we have acted on such lust.

Saved fallen created beings still in an incarnate state are most susceptible to attacks by Satan's mortal mind when they do not know what they are dealing with. When they do not know what they are dealing with, they can receive thoughts, feelings, ideas, words, images, and scenarios in their imaginations that they will mistakenly accept as their own. That is why spiritual hypervigilance is required for us to quickly identify the true source of the thoughts that we think and the emotions that we feel. We must learn to recognize thoughts and emotions that are not our own before we accept them and act on them — causing them, then, to become our own.

In order to successfully combat Satan's mortal mind, we need to identify if we have any resentment and unforgiveness toward others. One way to become aware of subconscious, or unconscious, resentment or unforgiveness is to fast. Fasting enables us to become more sensitive to God's Holy Spirit and the thoughts and ideas that He would lift up within our consciousness in order for us to become more aware of the existence and cause of — as well as solution to — our unclean desires. In contrast, long term physiologic satiety contributes to a type of mental lethargy that makes us less sensitive to some specific thoughts and ideas that God's Holy Spirit wants to impress upon us. (Long term physiologic satiety comes from sustained elevated blood levels of: (1) simple sugars and their breakdown byproducts, (2) fats and their breakdown byproducts, and (3) digestion-related hormones.) Those of you for whom twenty-four hour fasting: (1) is too difficult, (2) is against your doctor's orders, or (3) makes you feel ill can often achieve the same results by eating a normal lunch and, then, skipping an evening meal.

In sleep during a fast, God's Holy Spirit lifts up to our consciousness what He knows is needed in our awareness for successfully combating Satan's mortal mind. When God's Holy Spirit shows us that we have resentment and unforgiveness, then we need to work them out by: (1) focusing on them in continual prayer and confession, (2) examining the underlying reasons for them, and (3) forgiving others for their real or perceived wrongs against us. As soon as we successfully accomplish these three tasks through the guidance of God's Holy Spirit, we will be less susceptible to attacks from Satan's mortal mind and, then, we will be able to more effectively combat the thoughts, feelings, ideas, words, images, and scenarios that are imparted from demonic realms to the carnal mind of our lower, abased, or animal self.

Metaphysically speaking, thoughts, feelings, ideas, words, images, and scenarios from Satan's mortal mind are viral in that they can continuously mutate to escape detection, elude treatment, and replicate themselves furiously within us as well as "jump" to others through our negatively influencing them. That is why we must forever be on guard against Satan's mortal mind through spiritual hypervigilance in prayer and communion with God as well as through forgiveness of others in humility and gratitude. To be sure, we should not attribute every temptation and negative thought to Satan's mortal mind acting on the carnal mind of our old self, just 99.99%.

In addition to ongoing prayer and communion with God, successfully combating Satan's mortal mind calls for us to deepen our faith-walk with God by communicating our thoughts, feelings, and ideas to God at the same time that we ask for His perspective on them and take time to listen to His response. Living with God means living with God all of the time.

Anyone who is in the throes of active addiction to sin and sinful thoughts, feelings, ideas, words, images, and scenarios is not yet ready to successfully combat Satan's mortal mind. We need to be in recovery daily concerning our sinful interests and unclean desires.

In summary, in order to successfully combat Satan's mortal mind, we must accept that we will be bombarded daily by thoughts, feelings, ideas, words, images, and scenarios that play on the unclean desires of our heart. But we must never accept any of them as our own because, once we do, we will invariably act on them and make ourselves even more susceptible to demonic influences.

Pondering Victory

At the time of this edition (2022), there are five different battles that still need to be won:

1. The spirit of Antichrist must be overcome by, in, and through Christ Jesus.

The spirit of Antichrist is the spirit that deceives people into believing that God does not need to have an only-begotten Son, that Jesus Christ is not the only-begotten Son of God, and that Jesus Christ did not die for our sins. To be sure, it is the spirit of Antichrist that will motivate the end-time ruler known as *the Antichrist* to set himself up as the god of this world. Fortunately, Christ Jesus himself will have victory over the end-time Antichrist and will cast him into the Lake of Fire when he returns to begin his Millennial rule on Earth.

Fortunately, people who live during the Millennial rule of Christ Jesus will not have to contend with the spirit of Antichrist. The spirit of Antichrist will have been removed completely throughout Christ Jesus' Millennial rule.

At the time of this edition, the human being known as *the Antichrist* has not yet been identified, but his presence looms large on the horizon.

2. Our lower, abased, or animal self must be overcome by, in, and through Christ Jesus.

In order to overcome our lower, abased, or animal self, we must each learn to overcome carnal mind, which is the intellect of that self. It is in learning to overcome carnal mind — the mind of our fallen self and old sin nature — that we will have victory over all sinful desires and addictions to grandiosity, pomposity, brutishness, and vulgarity.

We can only have victory over carnal mind by depending on (1) God's divine Mind, (2) our Lord and Savior Jesus Christ, and (3) God's Holy Spirit. We cannot be self-disciplined and obedient to God if we do not rely radically on God as our universal Self.

It does not matter if we live in a flesh body before or during the Millennial rule of Christ Jesus on Earth, all human beings will continue to have unclean desires with which they must contend daily.

Before Christ Jesus returns bodily to Earth for his Millennial rule, the struggles that human beings have with carnal mind are compounded by Satan's mortal mind — which operates through Satan himself, his fallen angels, and his unclean spirits to play upon the mind of our fallen self and old sin nature. Satan's mortal mind fans the flames of all worldly desires within our carnal mind and entices us into a web woven entirely by a false sense of self, self-deception, and self-absorption.

During the Millennial rule of Christ Jesus on Earth, Satan and his mortal mind will be incarcerated for the full 1,000 year period (Revelation 20:2). During that period of time, some human beings will be enticed away from Christ Jesus by their own worldly, material, and fleshly personal desires. No longer will they be able to say: "The Devil made me do it." In truth, they must admit: "I acted solely on my own unclean desires to disobey God."

3. Our human, conscious functioning, or composite self must be overcome by, in, and through Christ Jesus.

Both carnal mind and the human mind are motivated by the desire to control situations, conditions, and other people but for different reasons and different ends. Carnal mind is motivated primarily by self-gratification. The mind of the human, conscious functioning, or composite self is motivated primarily by self-survival. The motivation of self-gratification is completely contrary to the motivation of pleasing God, our universal Self. And the motivation of human self-survival is completely contrary to the continuum and continuity of life that exists in God, our universal Self.

In order to have victory over the human, conscious functioning, or composite self, we must be willing to die daily to a false sense of self. We must become willing to give up our human lives, both figuratively and literally, in service to Christ Jesus. This is as true for those who live during the Millennial rule of Jesus Christ as it is for those who live before that rule.

We can have victory over the human mind if we are willing to live only for the good of all and the God of all, regardless of harmful consequences to our longevity or reputation. In the final analysis, we should desire to promote the Name of God rather than our own individual names!

4. Satan's mortal mind must be overcome by, in, and through Christ Jesus.

Human beings have to contend with Satan's mortal mind before the bodily return of Jesus Christ to Earth and, once again, at the end of the Millennial rule of Jesus Christ on Earth, when Satan is released from his incarceration in the bottomless Pit to incite World War IV by mounting the battle of Gog and Magog against Christ Jesus and the people of God (Revelation 20:7-8). That final battle will have all created beings firmly footed in either one of two camps: God's camp or Satan's camp. Fortunately, we know that the end of that battle will be with the final purge of Satan, who will be cast into the Lake of Fire for all eternity (Revelation 20:9-10).

5. Mortality, or physical death, must be overcome by, in, and through Christ Jesus.

Physical death will be the final enemy over which there will be complete victory by, in, and through Christ Jesus:

{22} For as in Adam all die, even so in Christ Jesus shall all be made alive. {23} But every person in their own order: Christ Jesus the firstfruits; afterward they that are Christ Jesus' at his return. {24} Then will come the end, when Christ Jesus shall have delivered up the kingdom to God the Father; when Christ Jesus shall have put down all [deviant] rule and all [divisive] authority and power. {25} For Christ Jesus must reign until God the Father has put all enemies under the feet of Christ Jesus. {26} The last enemy that shall be destroyed is death.

1 Corinthians 15:22-26 KJV Paraphrase [Author's Brackets]

In the previous passage, please note that there is a "fast forward" of 1,000 years from verse 23 to verse 24 — from the time of Christ Jesus' return (verse 23) to the time that Christ Jesus delivers his kingdom to God the Father (verse 24).

Victory over mortality, or physical death, will occur only after Satan has been thrown into the Lake of Fire and God has judged the remaining dead at the time of His Great White Throne Judgment, which precedes the formation of "a new heaven and a new earth" (Revelation 20:10-15; 21:1). At that time, all created beings who belong to God will be made of a new substance: the substance of God, our universal Self. (The present author wrote "remaining" because the first such transformation occurred for the saved in Christ Jesus at the time when he returned to Earth for his Millennial rule.)

After the formation of "a new heaven and a new earth," there will be no more battles to be won! The war will be over.

Exercises and Activities in Christian Metaphysics

1. If the Creator-God knew that we were going to fail and fall, why did He create us?

2. Because Adam and Eve fell, does that mean that they were created with flaws?

3. What is instantaneous about God becoming our universal Self and what is gradual?

4. How can you reconcile that God's Will is always in operation in His physical universe yet not always in operation in the souls of human beings?

5. Discuss natural disasters and disobedience to God's Will.

6. Is the conversion of potential energy to kinetic energy always harmful?

7. What always precedes a spiritual fall? (See Proverbs 16:18)

8. Can Satan or his fallen angels be redeemed? Why or why not?

9. What enables you as a saved fallen created being to produce fruit that glorifies the Creator-God?

10. Why are you regularly conflicted?

11. Sort out the differences in the states of being for each of the following four categories: (a) saved fallen created beings who are incarnate, (b) unsaved fallen created beings who are incarnate, (c) saved fallen created beings who are discarnate, and (d) unsaved fallen created beings who are discarnate. (Use terms such as

corporeality, incorporeality, mortality, and *immortality* as well as *Earth, Heaven,* and *Hades* in your answer to this question.)

12. Discuss differences between spiritual competition and spiritual cooperation.

13. As a saved fallen created being, what should be your greatest desire?

14. How can you achieve your greatest desire?

15. What is the identity of (a) Satan, (b) fallen angels, (c) unclean spirits, and (d) human beings who have committed the ultimate blasphemy?

16. Take time to craft an individual treatment plan for yourself that will help you to successfully combat thoughts, feelings, ideas, words, images, and scenarios that have their origin in Satan's mortal mind. (Do not share your treatment plan with others.)

17. What victories need to be won (a) before the Millennial rule of Jesus Christ, (b) during the Millennial rule of Jesus Christ, (c) toward the end of the Millennial rule of Jesus Christ, and (d) after the Millennial rule of Jesus Christ?

Chapter Seven

Every *Thing* is a Function of Consciousness

Every *thing* is a thought and every thought is a *thing*. Understood in this metaphysical context, a *thing* can be seen or unseen, visible or invisible, living or nonliving, animate or inanimate, corporeal or incorporeal, conceptual or nonconceptual, real or imaginary, and spiritual or physical. However, regardless of its individual attributes, every *thing* is a function of consciousness. That is what this chapter is about.

When many people think about or discuss consciousness, it is self-awareness that they are usually thinking about or discussing. Of course, self-awareness is subsumed within the general topic of consciousness, but self-awareness does not delineate the full extent of what consciousness is, especially when consciousness is viewed in the context of Christian metaphysics.

In the context of Christian metaphysics, consciousness is *true substance.* Yes, matter is the substance of the physical universe, but consciousness is the true substance of the entire universe (i.e., *das gesamte Universum* or *das ganze Weltall).* Every *thing* everywhere is a function of consciousness. Consciousness is the only real substance of the entire universe. Within the entire universe, spiritual things collectively constitute one domain and physical things collectively constitute their codomain. Both things and thoughts are inputs as well as outputs of consciousness.

As used here, "the entire universe" includes the so-called spiritual universe and the so-called physical universe because the two are interdependent, interwoven, and interdigitated throughout all-space and all-time. Even though an individual may speak or write about the spiritual universe and the physical universe as if they were separate, there really is only one universe. Mathematically speaking, the *entire universe* constitutes one whole and complete *set* that includes the spiritual universe and the physical universe as its subsets. In other words, the *entire universe* includes everything spiritual as well as everything physical and is synonymous with *all-that-is.*

Author's Note: For the sake of clarity, as used in the context of this book, *all-space* and *all-time* include (1) the absolute time and absolute space (i.e., absolute space-time) of eternity in the spiritual universe and (2) the relative time and relative space (i.e., relative space-time) of temporality in the physical universe.

The spiritual universe is a subset of the entire universe and the physical universe is a subset of the entire universe. The spiritual universe and the physical universe intersect as subsets to the highest order of $E = mc^2$, where E represents unbound energy and m represents bound energy. For human onlookers, the image of the domain of the spiritual universe is completely obscured by the image of its codomain, the physical universe. In other words, corporeality masks incorporeality. That is why, for human beings, the spiritual universe can only be seen and understood — that is, *apprehended* and *comprehended* — metaphysically.

In the context of Christian metaphysics, consciousness as true substance is the fabric of *all-that-is.* Consciousness constitutes every *thing* and every thought. Consciousness provides the substrate upon which everything spiritual or physical is constructed. Although every object is not self-aware, everything that exists in the entire universe is a manifestation of consciousness.

What is being presented here should not be confused with *pantheism.* *Pantheism* is the belief that the Creator-God inhabits every physical thing, including inanimate objects as well as animate beings. In a way, pantheists view all physical objects as transient emanations of divinity — regardless of the different verbiage they might use to express what is perceived as the Creator's connectedness to physicality. Pantheists conclude that the Creator-God can actually be found in physical things — not just in their design or essence but in the things themselves. (The grammatical construction "things themselves" is distinctly different from the metaphysical expression "things-in-themselves.") The title of this chapter, "Every *Thing* is a Function of Consciousness," is not meant to be pantheistic. It is meant to convey the idea that consciousness manifests every spiritual thing as well as every physical thing. The title of this chapter is not meant to convey the idea that everything is consciousness-in-itself or that the Creator-God inhabits physical objects or living things — the only exception, of course, is for people still in flesh bodies who have accepted Christ Jesus as their personal Savior and, therefore, have God's Holy Spirit indwelling their souls. (The Holy Spirit indwells each saved soul and each saved soul in corporeality resides in its own physical body.)

In the context of Christian metaphysics, consciousness is the pulsating substance from which everything is made. Consciousness provides the matrix upon which each spiritual thing is constructed. And consciousness provides the matrix upon which each physical thing, inanimate or animate, is constructed. Although everything physical is a manifestation of consciousness, consciousness-in-itself is tangible only to the metaphysical sense. Consciousness is not tangible to the physical senses; it is only through the metaphysical sense that we can perceive consciousness. In other words, it is only our metaphysical sense that can become conscious of consciousness. Although the metaphysical sense can be translated into brain neuroanatomic activity so that human beings can become knowledgeable of metaphysical truths, our metaphysical sense originates independently of our brain neuroanatomic activity. Although our physical senses can detect physical elements that might lead us to make metaphysical conclusions about the creation's intelligent design and causality, our metaphysical sense is essentially independent of our physical senses.

Consciousness can only stimulate the sense that it directly comes in contact with. Consciousness does not directly come in contact with our physical senses. Thus, knowledge of consciousness is generally limited to our intuitive, psychic, or metaphysical sense. The present author writes "generally" because, when the Supraconsciousness of God's divine Mind surrounds, enshrouds, or envelopes human beings, their thinking and understanding are elevated beyond their own intuitive, psychic, or metaphysical abilities to more fully apprehend and comprehend the things and thoughts of God.

Consciousness includes the Supraconsciousness of God's divine Mind that is accessible to: (1) unfallen created beings who are incorporeal, (2) saved fallen created beings still in flesh bodies, and (3) spiritually-restored created beings who have returned to incorporeality (i.e., redeemed souls who have already transitioned back to Heaven). *Consciousness* even includes the vampiric semi-consciousness of Satan's mortal mind that permanently owns the personal space of fallen created beings whose souls are beyond redemption or reclamation.

It is the vampiric semi-consciousness of Satan's mortal mind that seeks to encroach on the personal space of unsaved fallen created beings whose souls are not yet beyond redemption or reclamation (this includes some discarnate souls and some incarnate souls) as well as redeemed fallen created beings still in flesh bodies. Concerning the latter category, as long as redeemed fallen created beings remain in corporeality, they retain dual natures. When they transition from corporeality to incorporeality (i.e., from an incarnate state to a discarnate, heavenly state), redeemed souls then become immune to temptation because their personal carnal natures have ceased to exist.
Spiritual warfare exists in the universe between the Supraconsciousness of God's divine Mind and the vampiric semi-consciousness of Satan's mortal mind. This warfare is entirely spiritual. However, in the earth plane of consciousness, this warfare primarily takes place on the battlefield of the human mind. Daily, each human being is tempted by the vampiric semi-consciousness of Satan's mortal mind to consciously yield to it. Lamentably, even when the battle is over at the end of one day, the war continues the following day. Although a particular battle may be won, the war between Good and Evil will

never be completely over until Satan and all of his minions are finally cast into the Lake of Fire at the end of Christ Jesus' millennial reign on Earth.

The inanimate and animate objects in the physical universe provide evidence of a creation that has been cursed by the Creator-God in response to the errant actions of created beings who fell because they consciously (i.e., willfully) stepped outside of God's Will. Even though their Fall was the cause of the curse (i.e., our exile from Eden, Paradise, or Heaven), consciously stepping outside of the Will of God and the imposition of God's resultant curse were concomitant — that is, *simultaneous and synchronous.*

In the physical universe, matter represents the "thickened consciousness" of spiritual darkness conceived (i.e., manifested) by errant created beings at the time of their spiritual fall — which, because it was instantaneous, was really more of a *crash.* (Because the meaning of the word *fall* can include a drifting downward, or slow descent, the present author sometimes prefers the term *crash* over the term *fall* for the rapid downward spiral of Adamic beings who knowingly stepped outside of the Creator-God's Will.)

Consciousness excludes nothing but does not include everything. For example, the Supraconsciousness of God's divine Mind excludes the vampiric semi-consciousness of Satan's mortal mind. The Supraconsciousness of God's divine Mind is capable of such active exclusion because it possesses all-power (i.e., the only real power) and all-reality (i.e., the one true reality). At the time the vampiric semi-consciousness of Satan's mortal mind originated, it passively excluded itself from the Supraconsciousness of God's divine Mind because its nature is antithetical to the Nature of God.

Satan's mortal mind has no *real* power (i.e., no eternal power). Satan's mortal mind can only tell lies and create illusions in order to get created beings to turn their own power and dominion over to it. Metaphysically speaking, Satan's mortal mind seeks parasitic dominion over the consciousness of all life forms throughout the entire universe. Satan's mortal mind seeks parasitic dominion because it is in competition with the Supraconsciousness of God's divine Mind.

What imparts self-awareness to created beings with free will? Only the Supraconsciousness of God's divine Mind imparts self-awareness. Only the Creator-God is the author of all life and all real being. The vampiric semi-consciousness of Satan's mortal mind is a perversion of the original consciousness with which the Archangel Lucifer was endowed. The consciousness that Lucifer possessed was eternally poisoned when jealousy, envy, and hatred of the Creator-God originated within him.

Can consciousness in the context of Christian metaphysics be observed empirically from a human standpoint?

Yes, by observing the actions, reactions, and interventions of various forms of consciousness, including actions, reactions, and interventions within the physical universe from: (1) the Supraconsciousness of God's divine Mind, (2) angelic consciousness, (3) human individual and collective consciousness, and (4) the vampiric semi-consciousness of Satan's mortal mind. For the sake of clarity, the vampiric semi-consciousness of Satan's mortal mind manifests itself through the actions, reactions, and interventions of Satan, his fallen angels, and his demons, devils, or unclean spirits.

The meaning of the noun phrase *Christ Consciousness* has been trivialized in New Age philosophies. One cannot have Christ Consciousness without accepting Christ Jesus as one's personal Savior and without understanding the efficacy of his shed blood for the remission of one's sins. When understood correctly, the expression *Christ Consciousness* is synonymous with the expression *the Supraconsciousness of God's divine Mind* as well as the expression *the mind of Christ*. Indeed, Christ Consciousness is the consciousness that is found in the mind of Christ Jesus. No human being can have Christ Consciousness without recognizing Christ Jesus as the only-begotten Son of God as well as accepting him as one's personal Savior.

Because every *thing* is a function of consciousness, thoughts, images, concepts, and ideas can *bleed through* from one plane of consciousness to another. *For example,* thoughts, images, concepts, and ideas can *bleed through* from spiritual beings in a heavenly plane of consciousness to human beings in the earth plane of consciousness. And, within the earth plane of consciousness itself, thoughts, images, concepts, and ideas can *bleed through* from one human being to another.

For redeemed souls in Heaven, the phrase "bleed through" is ironic because, living fully in the shed blood of Christ Jesus (metaphysically, of course), they are able to easily communicate with one another. (When we live, move, and have our being fully in the shed blood of Christ Jesus, communication between and among souls who belong to God is crystal clear.)

Although redeemed souls in Heaven are able to communicate with redeemed souls on Earth, such communication is more difficult because of the constraints placed upon human beings by their corporeality as well as by their Creator. Also, the Creator places constraints on communication from Heaven to Earth because the Creator wants human beings to develop their individual faith and trust in Him as Creator-God, the source of all Life, and not shift dependence on Him to dependence on angels or saints in Heaven.

What is a *plane of consciousness* and what *planes of consciousness* exist?

As used by the present author, a *plane of consciousness* is a layer, level, stratum, or band of consciousness. Major planes of consciousness include: (1) the heavenly plane, (2) the terrestrial plane, (3) the interim plane, and (4) the hellish plane. (Each of these four major planes contains various substrata.) (1) The heavenly plane is the highest, deepest, and greatest plane of consciousness; the totality of God's divine Mind dwells within this plane of consciousness. (The consciousness of God's divine Mind can also be referred to as *the Supraconsciousness of God* and the spiritual space that it fills may be referred to as *God's spiritual universe*.) (2) The terrestrial plane is the plane of consciousness in which sentient beings live in physicality; for human beings, this plane may also be referred to as *the earth plane of consciousness*. (3) The interim plane of consciousness is the state of being where souls await physical birth. And (4) the hellish plane of consciousness is the state of being where unredeemable souls await their final judgment.

What is the dimensionality of consciousness?

Consciousness transcends dimensionality although consciousness can *push* its substantive reality into multi-dimensional states of being. *For example,* when God speaks as Creator or Judge, He can *push* His reality onto the axes, or dimensions, that are associated with physicality. The axes of physicality include these five vectors: (1) length, (2) width, (3) depth, (4) time, and (5) unified spatial force. (Because what to call the fifth dimension is still debated, the present author has chosen to call it "unified spatial force." As the present author sees it, "unified spatial force" unites quantum mechanics, wave theory, electromagnetism, and gravity.) These five vectors constitute relative *space-time,* which is subsumed within the all-space and all-time of the entire universe.

As mentioned earlier, the spiritual universe and the physical universe are subsets to the highest order of $E = mc^2$, *where E* represents unbound energy and m represents bound energy. Together, these subsets constitute *all-that-is,* or *the entire universe.* Since they are subsets of the entire universe, one can think of consciousness as the function that unites the spiritual universe to the physical universe. Conceptually, (1) every element in the spiritual universe has at least one corresponding element in the physical universe, and (2) every element in the physical universe has at least one corresponding element in the spiritual universe.

What is the difference between *structured* consciousness and *unstructured* consciousness?

The present author uses the qualifiers *structured* and *unstructured* to help distinguish creative consciousness in human beings that utilizes deductive and inductive reasoning (i.e., structured, or analytical, thinking) from creative consciousness that utilizes discernment (i.e., unstructured awareness).

Is it necessary to use the qualifier *creative* in conjunction with *consciousness* (i.e., *creative consciousness)?*

Using the qualifier *creative* in conjunction with *consciousness* helps to distinguish true consciousness from the altered consciousness of Satan, his fallen angels, and his unclean spirits, demons, or devils. Although the eternally fallen may devise cunning plans, such beings are not genuinely creative nor can they ever be (even though they were before their *crash).* Eternally fallen beings can only cast illusions and spin lies; they cannot actually create. It is impossible for anyone evil to actually create.

What is *altered* consciousness?

Before Lucifer's *crash,* the Supraconsciousness of God's divine Mind was the only consciousness that existed. That consciousness became altered in Lucifer and in his fallen angels and, eventually, throughout the entire Adamic race in its own fall. Although that consciousness is permanently altered for the eternally damned (Lucifer, his fallen angels, unclean spirits, and members of the Adamic race who have consciously rejected Christ Jesus as their personal Savior), that consciousness is only temporarily altered for members of the Adamic Race who eventually accept Christ Jesus as their personal Savior while they are still in corporeality. The operative words here are "while they are still in corporeality" because the Creator-God has decreed that salvation can only be received and experienced during one's sojourn in corporeality; salvation cannot be received and experienced while in a discarnate state.

In order to understand how we become one with the Creator-God, it is important for students of Christian metaphysics to recognize that the

Creator-God abides in us and we abide in the Creator-God through the consciousness we share. (The meaning of the verb *abide* here includes "to live, dwell, reside, continue, and remain" in each other.) It is through the consciousness we share that the Creator-God becomes our universal Self. And it is through the consciousness we share that we are not only made one with the Creator-God but also one with each other.

Throughout the entire universe, every holy thing is a function of the Supraconsciousness of the Creator-God and every holy thought in His creation is built on the matrix of His creation's desire to please Him by worshiping Him in spirit and in truth as well as in accomplishing His Will.

Exercises and Activities in Christian Metaphysics

1. Provide a dictionary definition for *consciousness* (remember to cite the source in your answer) and compare and contrast the dictionary definition with the way the word *consciousness* is presented in this chapter.

2. How do the *physical universe* and the *spiritual universe* relate to each other and to the *entire universe?*

3. Discuss the equation $E = mc^2$ and what its terms *(E, m,* and *c)* mean in the context of physics as well as in the context of Christian metaphysics.

4. Does the Creator-God inhabit inanimate objects and living things in the physical universe? Are there any exceptions?

5. If consciousness is not tangible to the physical senses, how can consciousness be observed empirically from a human standpoint?

6. Discuss the interrelationships of *the Supraconsciousness of God's divine Mind, angelic consciousness, human consciousness,* and *the vampiric semi-consciousness of Satan's mortal mind.*

7. In what way is *creative consciousness* distinguishable from the *altered consciousness* of eternally fallen created beings?

8. Why does each saved human being have dual natures? When does this duality come to an end?

9. Explain the meaning of the statement: "Consciousness excludes nothing but does not include everything."

10. What imparts self-awareness to created beings with free will?

11. How has the meaning of the noun phrase *Christ Consciousness* been trivialized?

12. Discuss the meaning of the phrase *bleed through* as it relates to the four major planes of consciousness.

13. According to the present author, what are the five axes (vectors) of physicality?

14. The following mathematical terms are used in this chapter: *set, subset, order, function, domain, codomain, input,* and *output.* Research their mathematical meanings and compare them to their meanings in the context of the Christian metaphysics discussed in

this chapter. Feel free to use graphic (i.e., diagrammatic) representations in your answer to this question.

15. Why does God place constraints on communication from saints in Heaven to saints on Earth?

16. How many major planes of consciousness exist and what are their names?

17. What is the dimensionality of consciousness?

18. What is the difference between *creative consciousness* and *altered consciousness?*

19. What is the difference between *structured consciousness* and *unstructured consciousness?*

20. How do we become one with the Creator as well as one with each other?

Afterword

At times, the words *gratification* and *satisfaction* may be used interchangeably. However, the nuances for *gratification* include responses from pandering to one's lower, animal, or abased self as well as responses from placating one's human, composite, or conscious functioning self. In contrast, the nuances for *satisfaction* include responses from honoring one's higher self, supraself, or absolute identity in God when something substantive has been produced with which one has personal identification. Although I am aware that few people will share my views on Christian metaphysics during my lifetime, I have experienced great satisfaction from being able to present them in this written work. Moreover, I am most grateful for the opportunity to present them to our Creator-God for His approval and possible use.

As a final note, I challenge each student of Christian metaphysics to do the following: Whenever instincts from your lower, animal, or abased self interact with emotions from your human, composite, or conscious functioning self to produce scenarios of temptation in your imagination, then actively replace the scenarios with views from your higher self, supraself, or absolute identity in God to overcome the temptation. Please understand this to be a lifelong challenge. Responding appropriately to this challenge is part of our daily toil while we remain clothed in human flesh (i.e., corporeality).

Appendix

Table One		
Strong's Number	**Hebrew Word**	**English Transliteration(s)**
H834	אֲשֶׁר	asher
H1961	אֶהְיֶה from הָיָה	eyeh from hayah
H3050	יָהּ	Yah, Jah
H3068	יְהֹוָה	Yahweh, Jehovah
H3091	יְהוֹשׁוּעַ	Y'hoshua, Yehoshua Jehoshua, Joshua
H3442	יֵשׁוּעַ	Y'shua, Yeshua Jeshua, Joshua
H4899	הַמָּשִׁיחַ from מָשִׁיחַ	H'Moshiach from Moshiach

Table Two	
Language	**Word in Brackets** (corresponds with the upper case "S" in *Self*)
Chinese	《自》
Korean	《본인》
Japanese	《自己》

BOOKS BY THE AUTHOR

As I See It: The Nature of Reality by God by Rev. Joseph Adam Pearson, Ph.D., Christ Evangelical Bible Institute, Copyright 2022. ISBN 978-0615590615.

Classroom Version of As I See It: The Nature of Reality by God by Rev. Joseph Adam Pearson, Ph.D., Christ Evangelical Bible Institute, Copyright 2022. ISBN: 978-1734294705.

God, Our Universal Self: A Primer for Future Christian Metaphysics by Rev. Joseph Adam Pearson, Ph.D., Christ Evangelical Bible Institute, Copyright 2022. ISBN 978-0985772857.

Divine Metaphysics of Human Anatomy by Rev. Joseph Adam Pearson, Ph.D., Christ Evangelical Bible Institute, Copyright 2021. ISBN 978-0985772819.

Hello from 3050 AD! by Rev. Joseph Adam Pearson, Ph.D., Christ Evangelical Bible Institute, Copyright 2022. ISBN 978-0996222402.

Christianity and Homosexuality Reconciled: New Thinking for a New Millennium! by Rev. Joseph Adam Pearson, Ph.D., Christ Evangelical Bible Institute, Copyright 2021. ISBN 978-0985772888.

The Koran (al-Qur'an): Testimony of Antichrist by Rev. Joseph Adam Pearson, Ph.D., Christ Evangelical Bible Institute, Copyright 2020. ISBN 978-0985772833.

Telugu Version of Quran: Testimony of Antichrist by Rev. Joseph Adam Pearson, Ph.D., Christ Evangelical Bible Institute, Copyright 2020. ISBN 978-0996222457.

Urdu Version of Quran: Testimony of Antichrist by Rev. Joseph Adam Pearson, Ph.D., Christ Evangelical Bible Institute, Copyright 2020. ISBN 978-0996222440.

Revelation of Antichrist by Rev. Joseph Adam Pearson, Ph.D., Christ Evangelical Bible Institute, Copyright 2021. ISBN 978-0996222488.

Intelligent Evolution by Rev. Joseph Adam Pearson, Ph.D., Christ Evangelical Bible Institute, Copyright 2022. ISBN 978-0996222426.

The Biology of Psychism from a Christian Perspective by Rev. Joseph Adam Pearson, Ph.D., Christ Evangelical Bible Institute, Copyright 2020. ISBN 978-0996222464.

The Threeness of God by Rev. Joseph Adam Pearson, Ph.D., Christ Evangelical Bible Institute, Copyright 2022. ISBN 978-1734294729.

To access free pdf editions of Dr. Pearson's books, visit:

http://www.christevangelicalbibleinstitute.com

or

http://www.dr-joseph-adam-pearson.com

ABOUT THE AUTHOR

Dr. Joseph Adam Pearson is a college and university educator with more than fifty years of classroom and administrative experience. Dr. Pearson has been the International President and Chief Executive Officer of Christ Evangelical Bible Institute (CEBI) for over twenty-five years. At the time of the latest publication of this book, he still oversees thriving branch campuses of CEBI in India, Pakistan, and Tanzania.

Currently, Dr. Pearson spends the majority of his time developing, designing, and deploying curriculum for Christian education nationally and internationally. And he preaches, teaches, and leads international crusades as well as provides group pastoral training in global mission settings.

During his professional life, Dr. Pearson has also served in the role of Senior Pastor of Healing Waters Ministries in Tempe, Arizona and as Dean of Instruction for Mesa Community College in Mesa, Arizona — where he was founding instructional dean for its Red Mountain Campus as well as Director of its Extended Campus.

Dr. Pearson holds a Bachelor of Science degree in Biology from Loyola University (Chicago), a Master of Science degree in Biology from Loyola University (Chicago), and a Ph.D. in Curriculum and Instruction with specializations in language, literacy, linguistics, and textual analysis from Arizona State University. He has also taken additional doctoral level coursework at the University of Chicago and at the University of Illinois Medical Center.

Dr. Pearson believes that after we are saved, and at the same time we are being sanctified, our individual lives and deeds are part of an "application" for the jobs that we will each hold during Christ Jesus' Millennial reign on Earth. Dr. Pearson's greatest goal is to be one of the many committed Christian educators who will be teaching during that period of time.

You may contact Dr. Pearson at drjpearson@aol.com or drjosephadampearson@gmail.com

www.ingramcontent.com/pod-product-compliance
Lightning Source LLC
LaVergne TN
LVHW081323060426
835511LV00011B/1827